Dealing with
Difficult
People

The Results-Driven Manager Series

The Results-Driven Manager series collects timely articles from *Harvard Management Update* and *Harvard Management Communication Letter* to help senior to middle managers sharpen their skills, increase their effectiveness, and gain a competitive edge. Presented in a concise, accessible format to save managers valuable time, these books offer authoritative insights and techniques for improving job performance and achieving immediate results.

Other books in the series:

Teams That Click

Presentations That Persuade and Motivate

Face-to-Face Communications for Clarity and Impact

Winning Negotiations That Preserve Relationships

Managing Yourself for the Career You Want

Getting People on Board

Taking Control of Your Time

A Timesaving Guide

THE RESULTS-DRIVEN MANAGER

Dealing with Difficult People

Harvard Business School Press

Boston, Massachusetts

Library of Congress Cataloging-in-Publication Data

The results-driven manager: dealing with difficult people.
  relationships.
      p.   cm. — (The results-driven manager series)
    ISBN 1-59139-634-4 (alk. paper)
      1. Problem employees. 2. Interpersonal conflict. 3. Personnel management. I. Title: Dealing with difficult people. II. Harvard Business School Press III. Series.
    HF5549.5.E42D428 2005
    658.3'045—dc22

                                                    2004010149

Contents

Contents

Contents

Dealing with
Difficult
People

Introduction

. . .

You can no longer deny it: Difficult people are everywhere, and as a manager you need to learn to deal with them. Whether direct reports or peer managers, difficult people and their frustrating behavior can take numerous forms. Chronic lateness or underperformance, irritability with customers, spats between employees, sniping via e-mails, and gossiping around the water cooler count among the more common versions. Persistent negativity—resisting needed change or shooting down new ideas, complaining constantly, and neglecting commitments—can also crop up in some workplaces. The more serious forms of difficult behavior include inappropriate comments from a manager to an employee that verges on harassment, sabotage of company equipment by a laid-off worker, or even physical attacks on others by an irate or disturbed employee.

Regardless of the form that difficult behavior takes, it exacts a serious toll on companies. Costs include high turnover and absenteeism, along with lowered productivity and morale. Distracted and frustrated by difficult behavior, managers have less time and energy to devote to their core responsibility: getting things done through others. All of this difficult behavior ultimately leads to one thing: damage to the company's bottom line.

Clearly, you can generate valuable results for your organization by dealing effectively with difficult behavior in the workplace. The payoff for these positive results ranges from increased job satisfaction, employee morale, and productivity to improved relationships with customers and rising profits. In addition, when you address difficult behavior skillfully, you free up more energy to invest in business-related projects—meeting deadlines more quickly and making fewer mistakes in the process. As an added bonus, you learn how to deal with difficult behavior that may present itself in the future. Put another way, you boost your ability to work productively with anyone, anywhere.

Part Art, Part Science

So where do you begin mastering this crucial managerial talent? You must start by making a distinction between behavior that calls for immediate dismissal of an employee—such as stealing or other outright illegal actions—and behavior that's problematic but not criminal. Your company's human resources department can provide you with further information on specific processes regarding these types of behaviors within your organization, as well as on how to recognize the distinctions between problematic and criminal behavior.

But a more daunting challenge remains: dealing with behavior that's not criminal but that *is* destructive to the company's operations and culture. After all, if you can't fire an employee for complaining or whining, what *can* you do? The answer lies partly in understanding the root causes and intense emotions that often lie behind difficult behavior—something we'll examine in greater detail in the sections that follow. In addition, you need to know how to adapt your response to the specific behavior in question. For instance, resolving a conflict between two employees requires a very different strategy than addressing a situation in which a worker has failed to follow through on a commitment. And that situation in turn differs from one in which an employee has shown persistent underperformance.

Managers who deal effectively with difficult people at work also possess an ability to reflect on their own behavior and attitudes—so as to discern whether they've played a part in causing the problem. Moreover, skilled managers are master communicators: They know how to deliver constructive feedback that helps others improve their behavior. And they have a talent for coaching, as well as for establishing a communication plan that prevents problematic behavior from even arising in the first place.

For all the reasons just noted, dealing effectively with difficult people at work is part art, part science. It takes a delicate blend of emotional savvy, interpersonal skill, and careful planning. In addition, you have to know how to address problem behavior *before* the situation translates into high turnover, absenteeism, flagging productivity, or sabotage. And, you need to identify when it's time to get outside help; for example, from anger-management specialists who can help defuse and channel the emotions that most often provoke difficult behavior.

The Force of Emotion

Although difficult behavior can stem from an innately annoying personality or from mental or physical health problems, most of it comes from strong emotions. These emotions include anxiety, anger, fear of loss, a desire to win arguments and to always be "right," and a need to feel competent, likeable, or important at the office. But what causes these turbulent emotions? Many of these volatile feelings have intensified over time owing to troubling workplace and societal trends.

For example, waves of downsizing have crashed across corporate America, leaving laid-off employees bitter and survivors fearful of losing their jobs in the wake. Technological advances and other profound changes, along with the demand from executives and corporate boards to "do more with less," have given people the sense that they've lost control over how their work gets done. Cost-cutting by corporations, including reductions in health-care coverage for workers, has many employees convinced that their company simply doesn't care for them any-more. The result? Profound anxiety, anger, and fear that get expressed through on-the-job apathy, resistance to change, and other problematic behaviors.

At the same time, changes in the larger society have only exacerbated the situation. We see depictions of anger and violence wherever we turn—from what we watch on TV or see at the movies, to the disturbing and upsetting reports we read in the newspaper or see on our computer or television screens while sipping our morning coffee. And that's not all: It's no secret that people as well as corporations have grown increasingly litigious in recent decades. Witness the rise in discrimination and harass-ment charges made by employees, along with the use of lawsuits to resolve disputes. Finally, globalization and the resulting diversity in the workplace can sometimes spawn frustration as managers and employees with diver-gent thinking and problem-solving styles lock horns over the best way to enhance productivity, compete against rival companies, or improve customer service.

To be sure, no manager can do much to eliminate the major business and societal changes that drive intense emotions in the workplace. Nor can you eradicate the feelings themselves. Instead, you need to focus your efforts on the behaviors involved (including your own), rather than on the personalities. Although it's easy to blame a *person* for being "difficult" and view problematic actions as the result of a character flaw, you'll get much better results if you approach the problem as one of *behavior*. As it turns out, it's a lot easier to influence someone else's actions than it is to transform his or her character or personality!

The articles in this collection are designed to help you do just that. The selections are organized into three parts and examine major themes that will help you to deal with difficult people: adapting your response to specific types of problematic behavior, exploring the impact of your own behaviors and attitudes on others, and communicating effectively about difficult behavior.

Let's take a closer look at these themes.

Matching Strategy to Specific Problem Behaviors

R. Brayton Bowen, who previously served as a senior officer with five *Fortune* 500 companies, starts things off in "Today's Angry Workplace" with a discussion of the business and societal trends that have increased anger, anxiety, and fear in the workplace. Bowen then recommends general strategies for dealing with these emotions. For example, he writes:

Every organization needs to have recognized protocols and processes for managing all levels of anger in the workplace. [These include] "no-tolerance" policies for addressing threats of violence; models for assertive communication that encourage employees to confront situations immediately and constructively *before* they get out of hand; and employee assistance programs (EAPs) for those conditions that are beyond the scope of managerial responsibility.

Bowen also advises firms to invest in training that focuses especially on assertive communications models and conflict management.

Sometimes, difficult behavior presents itself in a much less volatile way: An employee, for instance—though smart and highly skilled—is simply a "pain." The person aggravates everyone else with his or her prickly, domineering personality. Constantine von Hoffman explores this situation in "Crabs, Cranks, and Curmudgeons: How to Manage Difficult People." According to von Hoffman, managers can apply several strategies to deal with these types—including altering group dynamics. How? Ensure that each team includes a person with enough clout and personal presence to balance or neutralize a strong-minded member who runs roughshod over everyone else.

In "Don't Just Do Something—Sit There," business writer David Whitemyer proposes additional strategies for dealing with conflicts between employees. As it turns out, doing nothing may be your best tactic. By taking on disagreements between your direct reports and other employees, you lose the ability to focus on your own job and prevent employees from learning how to collaborate and communicate with one another directly. Instead of intervening, ask the person what he or she plans to do about the problem. Also, look for ways to use the conflict to improve group interactions. For example, if you point out that a disagreement represents differing viewpoints of people who all care deeply about what they're doing, the disputants may discover a new willingness within themselves to move past the conflict and begin communicating in more positive ways.

In addition to conflicts between employees, difficult behavior can express itself as persistent underperformance by workers. In "Will You Help or Heave Your Underperformers?" *Harvard Management Update* editor Paul Michelman tackles this challenge. Underperformance is particularly costly as more and more companies are forced to operate under tighter budgets, closer margins, and a pressing need to grow revenues. "Even the largest organizations," Michelman writes, can't be "carrying any dead weight." Michelman shares several experts' recommendations for addressing underperformance—including inviting the individual to provide his or her view on why performance is subpar, considering whether that person is in the position that best suits his or her skills, and clarifying performance expectations.

What about chronic failure to follow through on commitments? This additional form of difficult behavior can further burden managers and organizations that are struggling to boost financial performance. In "Consequences: The Secret to Holding People Accountable," the final article in this section, executive coach Lila Booth suggests a four-step process to help employees and teams define goals, commit to specific outcomes, monitor performance, and apply consequences for both good *and* less-than-stellar outcomes.

Evaluating Your Own Role in Problem Behavior

In the case of some difficult people, managers themselves may play a role in provoking the problem behavior. The articles in this section shed light on how to discern whether this is what's going on with your so-called difficult employees. For example, in "Don't Avoid Conflicts—Manage Them," Monci J. Williams argues that many managers duck an opportunity to go toe-to-toe with a difficult person because they view conflict as "bad" or as "warfare." But avoidance can spawn even more difficult behavior, because it leaves the underlying cause of the problem behavior unaddressed. Williams suggests ways to radically change the way you think about conflict. Begin viewing it as "the appearance of difference," she advises. You'll start seeing ways to explore and leverage those differences to "improve things that weren't working."

In "How to Handle Difficult Behaviors," conflict-resolution experts Ken Cloke and Joan Goldsmith provide additional guidelines for examining how your own attitudes about problem behavior can contribute to problem situations. They recommend asking yourself, for instance, whether you're overreacting to a difficult person simply because he or she reminds you of a troublesome family member. Cloke and Goldsmith also advise asking whether your own behavior is contributing to unproductive employee behavior. For example, are you letting complainers control group decisions, or promoting difficult individuals just to get rid of them?

In "When to Walk Away from a Fight," management writer Rebecca M. Saunders suggests that some managers get pulled needlessly into conflicts with employees because they have a strong need to be "right" or to be seen as the all-knowing, wise mediator of disputes. For managers who have such needs, Saunders lays out a method for determining whether it's in fact best to get into a shouting or "who's right" match—or if walking away would be wisest. Her recommendations include calculating the emotional investment that getting pulled into a "fight" would require. "Pause and ask yourself how much it would really matter—to the organization and/or yourself—if you won this difference of opinion," she writes. Saunders provides additional recommendations for keeping disputes productive if, upon reflection, you decide that jumping into the fray *is* worthwhile.

Author and management consultant Ronna Lichtenberg explores the tricky boundaries between work and life in "Five Questions About Business/Personal Relationships." As difficult as the balance can be, Lichtenberg suggests that you can actually have a genuine friendship with a colleague or business partner, as long as you pay attention to the potentially serious boundary issues and pitfalls. For those who have questions about how to initiate, monitor, and maintain multiple-role relationships, Lichtenberg has the answers.

Jamie Higgins and Diana Smith conclude the book's second section with "The Four Myths of Feedback," in which they define additional ways in which a manager's own attitudes may be contributing to an employee's problem behavior. These authors present four managerial misunderstandings about critical feedback that can worsen employees' performance problems—such as "My reality is *the* reality, and my job is to get you to see it," and "Mistakes are crimes to be covered up, punished, or both."

Communicating About Difficult Behavior

In addition to matching their responses to particular types of problem behavior and examining their own role in it, results-driven managers need to master the nuanced art of communicating with the individuals who are demonstrating difficult behavior. The articles in the third and final section of this book focus on this theme.

"Managing Negativity" starts things off with an examination of a particularly vital aspect of communicating about difficult behavior: understanding conflicting thinking styles among coworkers that can lead to disputes and destructive interpersonal tensions, and using those diverse styles to improve teamwork. Robert Bramson has identified five such thinking styles, as exemplified by five different types of people: *synthesists* are motivated by a desire to understand; *idealists* seek to reconcile differing opinions; *pragmatists* prefer concrete action to analysis and theorizing; *analysts* emphasize rational problem-solving processes; and *realists* see little need for synthesis, analysis, or compromise, because they believe the facts are readily apparent to everyone.

To capitalize on the "creative abrasion" that arises when people with different thinking styles work together, you must remain alert to the style mixtures that can prove the most "explosive." For example, synthesists are often natural debaters who love to ponder and argue a point. When synthesists are paired with pragmatists, whose chief concern is "getting on with the job," sparks can fly. If you see such tensions arise within your team, guide those sparks in the direction of company goals—and don't allow the players involved to set off personal attacks.

In "Checklist for Conducting a Disciplinary Conversation," Edward Prewitt provides guidelines for using communication to prevent problem behavior from arising in the first place—for example, by giving positive as well as constructive feedback and notifying employees as soon as you detect a hint of sagging performance. If problem behavior does arise, he recommends not taking action while you're angry. Wait until you've cooled down instead. Reprimand in private, and ask the person to explain the causes behind the difficult behavior. If the behavior persists, follow a standardized protocol comprising oral then written reminders, a suggested paid leave of absence, an ultimatum, and, as a last resort, termination of employment.

Author and teacher Beverly Ballaro suggests that employee evaluations are just as stressful for the reviewer as they are for the receiver. In "Performance Review Anxiety," she explores ways you can make them less painful and more productive. Ballaro helps lay out a plan of action that covers all the performance bases: accomplishments, goals, strategies, areas to improve, consequences, and incentives. Throughout the article, Ballaro emphasizes the importance of not just what you say, but how you say it. She writes, "it really is, as the saying goes, all in the delivery." Her tips will help you to reduce your own stress as you attempt to successfully communicate with a difficult person.

The next selection—"I Just Can't Bring Myself to Talk About That with Her."—presents the notion of communicating on three "levels" while discussing problem behavior. According to Douglas Stone, Bruce Patton, and Sheila Heen, such conversations must take place on a *factual* level ("What happened?"), a *feeling* level ("What are you worried about? What is making you feel defensive?"), and an *identity* level ("Am I being incompetent here?"). These authors advocate different communication strategies for each level; for example, "What's important to each of us?" (factual level), "I felt insulted when you said that" (feeling level), and "How do you perceive the situation and what do you consider is at stake here? " (identity level).

Your palette of communication skills for addressing difficult behavior also includes coaching—the use of one-on-one conversations to help others achieve desired, lasting changes in behavior. In "The Communication Secrets of Executive Coaches," business writer Nick Morgan draws from the field of executive coaching to highlight the most potent communication techniques for dealing with problem behaviors. One technique involves presenting a compelling vision to the person demonstrating the undesirable behavior. For example, suppose an employee has begun consistently submitting sloppily written proposals. In this case, instead of just telling the person to go back and redo a proposal, "explain how important the document is to the company, and *then* tell him to go back and redo it."

Morgan also advises managers to "commit to telling the truth. This is a prerequisite to having an effective conversation about change." Truth telling hinges on using appropriate vocabulary—that is, avoiding "pretense, jargon, 'spin,' and all the other ways in which we sugarcoat the sometimes hard things we need to say in order to create the right climate for change." When you let go of these devices, Morgan points out, "you [become] more attractive to others—because they will come to learn that they can trust you."

The last selection in this final part of the book, Hal Plotkin's "Feedback in the Future Tense," focuses on the question of how to frame constructive feedback during conversations with employees about problem behavior. The goal, Plotkin writes, is to focus not on past behaviors but on desired behavioral change in the future. Plotkin lays out a six-step process for facilitating feedback. Start by identifying specific employee successes and failures in concrete terms, he advises; for example, say to someone who is on the verge of becoming a chronically late employee, "You've come in late seven times in the last month." Then listen carefully to how this person responds to your observations and explains his or her views on the problem. When people feel that their views have been heard, they find it easier to take in and respond to others' viewpoints as well.

Plotkin also recommends presenting the implications of changing and not changing the identified behavior. Point out occasions when the person has been successful in the past, he suggests, and explain how "the traits that led to those successes can be applied to areas that need improvement." Then agree to an action plan, inviting the employee to suggest steps he or she can take to address the identified issues. Finally, follow up by setting "a date and time to meet again for a formal review on the progress related to the action plan."

Through it all, don't forget to communicate your appreciation for what the person has done well. Words of thanks, a note of commendation put in the employee's personnel file, and even a surprise day off can go a long way toward cultivating people's dedication to doing—and behaving—better.

Next Steps

As you've probably already surmised, dealing with difficult people in the workplace presents unique and daunting challenges for managers. Problematic behavior stems from complex emotional forces and expresses itself in numerous forms, each of which requires specialized strategies. In addition, a manager's own attitudes and behaviors—discomfort with conflict, a desire to be right, a tendency to make a dispute about personality and character rather than behavior—can further complicate the situation.

But an understanding of the forces behind difficult behavior, combined with a little self-reflection and communication know-how, can help any manager to transform problem behavior into valuable results for his or her company. It isn't easy, and it takes lots of practice. You've taken the first step by picking up this book. After you've read the selections that make up this volume, try putting your new knowledge into action to start generating valuable results for your organization. Ask yourself what difficult behavior is costing your company now, and what changes you can make to begin translating problem behavior into bottom-line gains for your firm in the future. Where will you start, and with whom? Which of the concepts and techniques in this book seem to offer the highest potential for positive change in your team, department, or company?

By applying the techniques described in this book, you'll not only benefit your company; you'll also sharpen your own skills and help those supposedly "difficult people" realize their full potential. Everyone wins.

What Types
of Difficult
People Must
You Deal With?

• • •

Difficult people can come in a bewildering array of types. Some are angry, anxious, or fearful about company policies or changes, while others constantly annoy you and their colleagues with their domineering or obnoxious personalities. Still others get into frequent disputes with one another on the job or regularly turn in subpar performance. And then there are those individuals who continually fail to follow through on commitments.

Each difficult person and his or her particular form of difficult behavior presents unique challenges for the hapless manager. If *you're* dealing with one or more of these types of people, don't despair. The articles in this section lay out potent strategies for handling even the more extreme forms of problem behavior. First, you'll learn how to discover the root causes behind the anger, anxiety, and fear that can lead to so much of the difficult behavior found in today's workplace—as well as tactics for managing these volatile emotions. You'll then find numerous suggestions for ways to address chronically annoying personalities and conflicts that all too often erupt between employees, as well as how to handle persistent underperformance and failure to honor commitments.

Today's Angry Workplace

An Interview with
R. Brayton Bowen

•   •   •

Prior to becoming a consultant, speaker, and writer, R. Brayton Bowen served as a senior officer with five *Fortune* 500 companies, including Federated Department Stores and Capital Holding Corporation (now AEGON). When he began consulting, in 1991, he became concerned with "the changing relationship between employers and employees and its impact on worker attitudes and morale." The concern led to research, and the research eventually led Bowen to produce and host a five-part documentary called "Anger in the Workplace" for the Public Radio

Partnership in Louisville, Kentucky. "This is an area that the major media have not given enough attention to," says WFPL program director John Gregory, who collaborated with Bowen on the series. "As we prepared these programs, I found that my own awareness as a manager was growing. I found that workplace anger can be a major issue just about anywhere."

Bowen interviewed scores of people, from authorities on employee attitudes to victims of downsizing, discrimination, even attempted homicide. He spoke to *Harvard Management Update*'s Tom Brown about what he found.

Is anger a bigger problem in the workplace today than it used to be?

The emotion of anger is certainly no stranger to the American workplace. But a number of factors—downsizing, changing technology, and the charge to "do more with less"—are contributing to heightened anxiety and, in turn, raw anger. Moreover, anger is increasing in society. Just turn on the TV to see anger and violence presented as regular entertainment. Get into heavy traffic to experience road rage, or pick up the papers to read about violence visited on school children by other children. Small wonder that homicide accounts for the highest percentage of job deaths and "going postal" is a new catchphrase.

Are these impressions supported by hard data?

There were 856 homicides reported in the workplace last year—more than twice the number reported a dozen years ago. Security experts report that "work rage" in the form of sabotage is on the increase. One telephone company experienced $10 million in damaged equipment at the hands of an angry former employee. Computer viruses are being created regularly to attack corporate and government systems. Charges of discrimination, harassment, and intimidation are rising. And litigation is becoming increasingly common for settling conflicts between employers and employees.

But surely people have always been unhappy at work.

Certainly. But the manner of expression was often more concerted, more organized. If you were a member of a union and got angry at the boss, you could file a grievance. If you were angry at the company, you could go on strike or engage in a slowdown. Today, there are fewer recognized conventions or systems for processing anger, so individuals are often taking matters into their own hands, and the manner of expression is not always rational—or pretty.

What do you think causes the intensity of today's anger?

In adults, anger is often triggered by the threatened loss of something greatly valued. Work, love, and play represent the triad that affect one's sense of well-being. The loss, or threat of loss, of any one of these gives rise to adult anger. Translate this to the workplace, and I'd rank these three factors as the biggest causes of anger: downsizing, or the threat of job loss; the pressure to do more with less, or the loss of existing resources; and disempowerment, or the loss of control over the work to be done.

How important an issue is downsizing, given today's record-low unemployment levels?

Consider the number of jobs lost due to downsizing. My statistics indicate that 1998 was a record year for job loss—almost 600,000—with 1999 predicted to be even worse. Just after last Thanksgiving, corporations announced more than 77,000 planned layoffs. And while three jobs are created for every one lost, many new jobs are at significantly lower levels of income. Indeed, the middle class is shrinking and the poor are getting poorer.

It used to be that downsizing was what companies did only when in deep trouble. Today it's a commonplace practice, even if companies appear to be doing well—although research indicates the long-term performance of organizations going through such Draconian measures is seldom, if ever, improved. What's key is that even the threat of downsizing can dramatically increase workplace anxiety.

What about the other causes you mentioned?

Workplace practices and policies are also having an impact. Even with all the rhetoric of people being "our most important resource," discrimination, harassment, and organizational takeaways are adding gasoline to smoldering embers. Loss or restriction of benefits like retirement and medical benefits add to the economic uncertainties of workers. Also, practices that in effect rob employees of their voice and sense of personal dignity—like leaving them out of decision-making processes or omitting them from important communications—add to the feelings of frustration and rage.

You've mentioned "anger" and "rage." Are they the same?

It's a matter of degree. I'm advocating that managers deal with situations before they result in employee turnover, absenteeism, poor productivity, and sabotage. Anger is expressed in many ways, not just in active aggression. The air-traffic controllers' by-the-book slow-down of air traffic during the Reagan administration was a classic case of "passive" aggression. No one was harmed personally, but the entire system was brought to a crawl. Today's volatile workplace is a different kind of environment, where individuals can act—unexpectedly, unpredictably, and with grave consequences—toward a targeted manager or company. When anger is uncontrolled and turns to hurting someone or physical destruction, it has crossed over to rage.

Can managers do anything about intense, combative anger?

Absolutely. First, they need to have a plan for dealing with such situations. Second, they need to know how and when to recognize the need for outside help. Third, they need to be proficient at employee relations and as skilled as possible in interpersonal effectiveness. Just as defensive driving requires each person to be accountable and responsible for driving safely, managing "offensively" requires each manager to be equally accountable and responsible for managing professionally, fairly, and proactively.

Furthermore, every organization needs to have recognized protocols and processes for managing all levels of anger in the workplace:

- "no-tolerance" policies for addressing threats of violence;

- models for assertive communication that encourage employees to confront situations immediately and constructively *before* they get out of hand; and

- employee assistance programs (EAPs) for those conditions that are beyond the scope of managerial responsibility.

Finally, companies need to invest more in supervisory development and interpersonal-effectiveness training of both supervisory and nonsupervisory personnel. Employees don't hang their emotions up with their hat when they come to work. Every employee brings his or her whole self to the job. Managers need to focus on this whole person, not just on task performance.

Maybe today's angry workplace needs some anger specialists.

It already has some. There are professionals involved in the area of "anger management" who tend to focus on the manifestations of the problem. And there are a few others who are beginning to work on the root causes. I never would have thought of myself as an anger specialist, but much of the work I do relates to making unhealthy environments less toxic.

Profiles in Anger

R. Brayton Bowen

Talking to people these days about what's going on in their workplace is an exercise in candor. Even people maimed by workplace violence are generally approachable and open about their encounters and their feelings. Their testimony has left an indelible imprint on my view of employees and employers at the end of this century. Some of the most memorable people I talked with are profiled here.

- Tom had worked for a *Fortune* 50 life insurance company as regional manager for more than 20 years and said he had taken a sales territory from "dead last" to one of the "top 5" in the country. Moments after the new vice president landed, Tom was told his office was being closed. As Tom drove from the airport, he asked, "What about me?" The answer he said he received was chilling: "You've been 23 years with the company. You've got a wall full of plaques. We've paid you well, and we owe you nothing!"
- Ann related that she was "downsized with the greatest group of people you could ever want to be with—we were all 'toasted' on the same day. I was really proud of us as a group; we supported each other to the bitter end." A former employee of a large financial services company, she recounts, "I was there for 16 years. Even though I've been away for almost a year, I have residual anger, but it's towards the senior management of the company. It's my view they didn't have a grasp of what needed

to be done to take the company to the next level—they decided to sell while their shares were still worth something. And we were toast."

- **Buddy,** a health insurance employee, volunteers, "I've actually been downsized and rehired by my current employer three times." With respect to loyalty, he adds, "It's dead. Just forget it. In fact, it's not unusual in my company for employees to get an e-mail about the elimination of their job, with a request they call for an appointment to discuss their 'termination' package."

- **Jan,** who worked for an East Coast utility, recalls, "On the last day, I went in, did my thing, cleaned off my computer, walked out the door, and that was it . . . anticlimactic, except that my coworkers were very upset. We had worked together for almost 12 years. It was very emotional—difficult, very difficult—something I wouldn't want to go through again. I hope never to work for another corporation. I won't place my future in someone else's hands."

How do workers like these see anger in the larger context? Tom says, "I think there's a lot of anger in the workplace. Once you become a victim of downsizing, you need to feel that anger, go into a closet and explode, throw a chair against the wall, whatever you want to do—but feel that anger, let it out, just let it rip. Then hide it! You've got to let that anger work for you without showing it. But the corporate community is fooling themselves if they think the masses out there are not angry and that they all love their jobs."

Despite Tom's advice, very few I talked with seemed able to conceal their growing anger.

Do managers need to manage their own anger, as well as the anger of their employees?

That's very relevant! In fact, middle managers have been the principal focus of corporate downsizings. And those left behind are literally caught in the middle between the decision makers who are tightening the screws and the nonsupervisory personnel who are experiencing the brunt of change. I have found that many managers not only sense the frail employment status of their employees, but in case after case the manager shares it. This makes for a very awkward situation in which managers are often asked by the corporation to take actions they personally don't agree with. Needless to say, this just increases the anger level of the manager. It's not a healthy situation.

But surely managers are not wholly powerless.

Much of what impacts the organizational level of anger is manageable at the senior levels of the organization, where the values and cultures are shaped and key decisions made. It becomes more difficult as you go further out into the organization, where managers must implement decisions. However, every manager not only can but must do things—lots of things—to affirm personal worth, self-esteem, care, and concern. In fact, just as managing relationships is critical to successful marketing, managing employee relationships is an absolute imperative within the organization.

In summary, then: the major to-dos for a manager?

First: Develop a plan for anger management, including establishing policies, retaining employee assistance program counselors, and identifying special resources in advance to assist with crisis situations.

Second: Invest in more training and development; focus especially on assertive communications models, supervisory skills training, and human relations training. Build skills from top to bottom on how to manage conflict.

Third: Coach, train, and develop yourself and your employees to become independent agents, specialists who add value to whatever assignment they're on and who can become "quick-change artists," learning to adapt to new situations readily, even if it means going elsewhere. The more confident people are within themselves and with others, the more likely they will be able to work through the anxiety of change.

A last question. After two years of research on this topic, what surprised you the most?

I was surprised by the number of experts—think-tank professionals, professors from graduate schools of business, and consultants—who confirmed that anger is a growing concern. It's real. The experts agreed that mismanagement of anger has an extremely high cost associated with it. I might add it was sadly surprising that many victims of downsizing confided they would *never again* give deep commitment and loyalty to another corporation. How tragic!

So the "we employ you one day at a time" culture may be backfiring.

Loyalty in the past meant almost blind obedience to the company. What I'm talking about is being committed, as in a relationship, one to another. Where there is trust, great things can be accomplished. Pervasive anger has created a norm of noncommitment between employers and employees. The motto for both seems to be: "I'll use you, but I won't be abused." Business has brought this upon itself; the increased use of short-term, contingent, project-related employees has underscored the throw-away society in which we live. Employees are seen as disposable commodities in practice, rather than the cherished resources CEOs insincerely speak of.

For Further Reading

Anger at Work by Hendrie Weisinger (1995, William Morrow and Company)

The Assertive Advantage: A Guide to Healthy and Positive Communication by Sharon Anthony Bower (1994, National Press Publications)

The Human Equation: Building Profits by Putting People First by Jeffrey Pfeffer (1998, Harvard Business School Press)

Preventing Workplace Violence by Marianne Minor (1995, Crisp Publications)

Reprint U9902B

Crabs, Cranks, and Curmudgeons

How to Manage Difficult People

• • •

Constantine von Hoffman

The signs are everywhere: voices raised in the conference room, hushed conversations in the hall, closed-door complaints from employees on your team. One of the other people in the group—*yes, one of the smartest, most highly skilled people you have*—is a pain. A troublemaker. Someone who aggravates everybody and pleases nobody. Managers have always had to deal with problem employees, but in today's labor market you may not be able to boot your talented-but-difficult curmudgeons out the door. So what do you do?

Some of the possible solutions are straightforward, though often overlooked. But if these are inadequate, you can turn to the practitioners of a concept called *emotional intelligence* (EI) for help.

Wrong Job

To begin, check whether the troublesome employee is in the wrong job. "Is the person mismatched for the role they're in, for the personality they have?" asks Thomas Rice, CEO of Interaction Associates, an international consulting firm based in Cambridge, Massachusetts. "For example, often you'll find someone who is an introvert and a loner, maybe a highly intuitive kind of person who doesn't follow through administratively. Yet now they're expected to do all that kind of thing." This kind of mismatch occurs more frequently as technically skilled people are promoted into managerial roles, says F. Norris Dodge, president of H.R. Masters in Owings Mills, Maryland. "I'm finding people with low people skills now in people positions. The CPA or the analyst is now running the department. These are the very things that they were running away from—they wanted to work with numbers or machines—and all of the sudden they're trying to create teams and foster teamwork, and they don't have a clue."

If this is the problem, get your curmudgeons some managerial training quickly—or transfer them to jobs that better use their skills.

Job Requirements

Next, check whether the job itself requires them to be difficult. Some organizations have killer roles, positions that always seems to be occupied by cranks. Interaction's Rice gets suspicious whenever a person who zoomed from entry level to VP is now considered a pain in the butt. "I inquire into a bit of the history. What happened to the last person in this role—were they a pain in the butt too? 'Well, yeah.' And how about the one before that? 'Well, yeah, come to think of it, they didn't last too long. . . .'" Clearly this person is doing someone else's dirty work. "They're usually covering for someone—the president or somebody like that," says Rice.

What to do? Live with it. Acknowledge that being difficult is part of what you are asking such people to do. Rotate them out of the position before they burn out and leave.

Group Dynamics

Assess the group dynamic, which may itself be the villain. Organizations that are growing fast—and those with a demanding performance environment—often develop a leadership vacuum. The vacuum lets one strong-minded person run roughshod over everyone else. "You can get a very talented person in that situation who can be terrible and vicious . . . because you have a very dysfunctional group dynamic," says Rice. If that's the problem, make sure that every group includes at least one person with the personality or the clout to neutralize your prima donna.

Beyond Organizational Tinkering

These problems are organizational and can be solved relatively easily, provided you have the authority to make the necessary changes. But other problems are personal and interpersonal, the kind that are described in the catchphrases "personality clash," "bad chemistry," or "he rubs me the wrong way." Troublesome employees themselves may have difficult personalities. Or you, as the manager, may somehow be aggravating the situation by dint of your own personality rather than improving it. Whatever the specifics, emotional intelligence may hold the key to the solution.

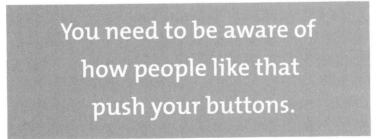

You need to be aware of how people like that push your buttons.

The basics of this concept have been spelled out by Daniel Goleman, author of two books on the subject (see box "Using Emotional Intelligence"). A person with

Using Emotional Intelligence

Emotional intelligence, writes Daniel Goleman, is "the capacity for recognizing our own feelings and those of others, for motivating ourselves, and for managing emotions well in ourselves and in our relationships." People with high levels of emotional intelligence (EI) can deal with problem employees more easily—and can avoid becoming problem employees themselves.

So can EI be learned? Absolutely, says the author, but not through conventional assembly-line classroom techniques. Rather, the learning has to be tied to an individual's strengths and weaknesses—and has to be reinforced with changes in behavior over time. And it often works best if it's self-directed. For example, an accountant described by Goleman recognized that she tended to flare up in anger when criticized "and said things she felt ashamed about later." Enrolled in an executive M.B.A. program, she decided to confront her weakness head-on through a series of steps including:

high EI is self-aware, self-confident, and able to empathize with other people. He or she is also adept at communicating, leading, and developing others—skills that not every manager possesses in abundance. "A lot of times [troublesome] people don't get better because their bosses don't have very much emotional intelligence in the way they manage them," says Cary Cherniss, a professor at Rutgers University's Center for Applied Psychology and director of the nonprofit Emotional Intelli-

- **Learning and mastering** techniques "for better self-control, such as anticipating hot-button situations and preparing herself so that she won't 'lose it.'" Reminding herself that most criticisms are actually "feedback that is meant to be helpful."
- **Practicing** and mentally rehearsing these responses as often as possible.
- **Role-playing difficult situations** with fellow students so she could "try out new self-control strategies."
- **Asking for reminders** from a fellow team member, who agreed to signal her when he saw her "being stubborn, inflexible, or otherwise overreacting."

Skills such as these, notes Goleman, are increasingly being taught in business schools—notably the Weatherhead School of Management at Case Western Reserve University, which designed an entire course to teach personal and emotional competencies.

gence Consortium, which is assembling a catalogue of best EI practices. "[Managers] need first of all to be aware of their own emotional responses and how people like that push their buttons. They have to be able to control their temper and their fear, depending upon what their situation is with that individual. They need to be confident and assertive in the way that they work with people like that—not intimidated or overwhelmed, but at the same time empathic and diplomatic."

What does this mean in practice? An emotionally intelligent manager might not try to change difficult employees' behavior directly, for example; instead, the manager would help employees understand the problems they're causing. "[Difficult] people . . . frequently are very low in self-awareness," says Cherniss. "If they are made aware of the impact that they have, then often they'll change." He cites the case of one overbearing, intimidating manager who kept claiming he was fine and didn't know why people were so upset. "Finally they videotaped him at a meeting—and when they showed him the videotape, tears came to his eyes. He just had no idea what he was like until he actually saw himself on the videotape."

Another useful tool: 360-degree feedback, in which people's performance is assessed by everyone around them (see the article, "Should You Use 360° Feedback for Performance Reviews?" *Harvard Management Update*, February 1999). "It's often misused," Cherniss says. "But when it's done as part of a development process, someone like an executive coach sits down with the individual and shares the information with that person in an emotionally intelligent way. . . . It can be very powerful in motivating change."

If acquiring these skills sounds daunting, the good news is that emotional intelligence can be learned. American Express Financial Advisors has been running an Emotional Competence training program for managers since 1992. A major goal is to help managers become "emotional coaches" for the people who report to them. The training helps managers appreciate the role that emotion plays in the workplace and develop a greater awareness of their own emotional reactions. It includes training in self-awareness, self-regulation, empathy, and social skill. Interestingly, these soft skills translate into hard results. A recent study found that trained managers grew their businesses by an average of 18.1% compared to 16.2% for untrained managers. That came to an estimated $247 million in increased revenue over the 15-month study period. Pam J. Smith, whose title is program manager for emotional competence, says that the company has also recorded greater retention and lower absenteeism as a result of the program.

No one is ever "sent" to the program, says Smith; it isn't used remedially. Even so, she adds, it can ease problems with difficult people by letting managers see where they themselves are causing or exacerbating the problems. Sometimes that's enough.

For Further Reading

Emotional Intelligence: Why It Can Matter More Than IQ by Daniel Goleman (1997, Bantam Books paperback)

Executive EQ: Emotional Intelligence in Leadership and Organization by Robert K. Cooper and Ayman Sawaf (1998, Perigee paperback)

Working with Emotional Intelligence by Daniel Goleman (1998, Bantam Books)

Reprint U9906B

Don't Just Do Something— Sit There

．　．　．

David Whitemyer

An employee storms into your office complaining about the new VP. She's fuming. You wonder how you can help.

Many managers' tendency would be to dive headfirst into this situation. As a manager, it's your job to solve problems and put out fires, right?

Not so fast. Have you considered doing nothing at all? Given the prevalence of terms like *harassment, anger management,* and *employee grievance* in the American workplace, one would hope that companies have a heightened awareness about the way people treat one another. But alas, one downside of the current situation is that many employees choose to let their supervisors settle disputes instead of handling them on their own.

> ## Ask yourself: How can this conflict best be used to improve the interactions in this group?

That creates two significant problems. First, managers' schedules are now squeezed tighter than ever. "Most managers spend much more time dealing with subordinates' problems than they even faintly realize," write William Oncken, Jr., and Donald L. Wass in the classic *Harvard Business Review* article "Management Time: Who's Got the Monkey?" One study found that 42% of the time of the managers surveyed is spent dealing with office conflict. Second, if managers never allow employees to work out conflicts among themselves, they'll never meld into a high-performing unit. At some point, subordinates have to learn how to collaborate and communicate directly.

In other words, not jumping in to resolve every employee tiff can benefit you the manager and your direct reports alike. "Intervening is a strategy, just like not intervening is a strategy," says Christine Kutsko, president of The Capstone Group, a consulting firm that specializes in performance improvement. Your decision to

Times When You Should Definitely Intervene

- When the disagreement is between an assertive employee and a timid, less vocal person, or when the rank of the disputants is not commensurate.
- When an argument between two employees has broadened to encompass additional staff members.
- When the conflict involves illegal conduct, such as sexual harassment or civil rights violations.

intervene—or not—should be the result of considered thought, not an emotional response to conflict. After all, conflict often occurs among people who care about what they're doing. Perhaps, instead of ending the dispute as quickly as possible, your chief concern should be: How can this conflict best be used to improve the interactions in this group?

"If a dispute doesn't interfere with an employee's performance, does not disrupt the work environment, and is not a violation of company policy, then 'benign neglect' is probably a suitable approach for a manager," says David Lipsky, director of the Institute on Conflict Resolution at Cornell University. View such a dispute as an opportunity for your staff members to develop their problem-solving skills. Even though you may be "doing" nothing in such a situation, it's crucial that you be "actively passive," advises management consultant Joan

Lloyd. As a general attitude and as a response to specific employee disagreements that you're aware of, you need to convey the perspective "that employees resolving their own conflicts is a development opportunity."

So, to return to the example of the direct report who's complaining about the new VP, don't try to referee the issue the employee is presenting. Instead of asking the direct report what she would like you to do, ask what she is planning to do.

Of course, not all employees feel experienced enough or confident enough in their position in the company to take this on. You need to be familiar with the maturity and communication style of your employees in order to determine your response. But in general, "if you treat employees with respect, if they feel like they are trusted to do the right thing, more often than not, they will have the confidence to resolve most issues that come up during workplace conflicts," says Matthew Gilbert, author of *Communication Miracles at Work* (Conari Press, 2002).

Reprint U0212E

Will You Help or Heave Your Underperformers?

Paul Michelman

You simply can't tolerate underperformance. Budgets are too tight, margins are too close, and the need for growth is too overwhelming for even the largest organizations to be carrying any dead weight.

For overburdened executives, often the first instinct is to drop underperforming managers. After all, who has the bandwidth to deal with them? "Underperformers take an inordinate amount of energy to manage," says Jim Bolton, CEO of Ridge Associates, a communications consulting firm. "You not only have to manage *their* performance, but, as chronic offenders, they become problems in *your* performance."

Look Before You Leap

Firing and replacing key managers is an arduous and time-consuming task. Not only is the separation process fraught with pain and risk, but according to Michael Watkins, Harvard Business School professor and author of *The First 90 Days* (Harvard Business School Press, 2003), the manager you hire may take six months or more before she produces any value.

Thus many executives don't confront problem behavior at all, Bolton says, "They find workarounds: they avoid the person, they're vague in giving feedback, and they often end up with more work to do in trying to compensate for these underperformers. One executive I worked with reorganized his 1,000-person division so he could make an underperformer someone else's problem," he says. "But ultimately the choice comes down to fish or cut bait."

In making that choice, experts say, you owe it to yourself, your organization, and to the manager in question to take at least one shot at diagnosing and addressing the underlying causes of unsatisfactory performance— especially if the employee has shown value in the past. To do so, consider this advice from the experts.

Diagnose and Prescribe

Before you can solve the dilemma of an underperforming manager, you need to establish the details of the problem. Begin by carefully evaluating the manager's results. "What is the manager doing or not doing?" asks John Baldoni, the author of several books on leadership. "Is he making the numbers? If not, why not?"

Next, Baldoni says, look at 360-degree results if you have them. "What are peers, bosses, and employees saying about the manager?" You should also do your own 360, asking key stakeholders and peers about the manager's performance.

In addition, Baldoni suggests asking the manager to provide his view on why his performance is subpar. "The reasons could vary from lack of support from you (the boss); inadequate resources in people, budget, and time"; to myriad other factors. "The manager may also be facing problems outside the office with spouse, children, or parent care."

Then consider talent/skill fit: "Ask yourself if this manager is in the right position," Baldoni says. "Does he have the right talent to do the job as well as the skills to perform? Talent you cannot coach; skills you can develop."

According to Joseph Weintraub, a professor of management at Babson College, performance issues with managers most often "revolve around a common lack of understanding of expectations between managers and their bosses." One way to diagnose this, he says, is to ask the manager to write down the "three most important things that they get paid to do. Then the manager's boss would independently do the same exercise for the manager."

After both have finished the exercise, they would compare results. "In the majority of cases, the lists look dramatically different, with a 'hit rate' of about one out of three expectations in common," Weintraub says. "With this data, the boss and manager can align expectations more clearly to help the manager to focus on doing the 'right things.'"

Give Solutions Reasonable Time to Take

Bolton cautions executives to maintain realistic expectations for a turnaround in performance. "It takes six weeks or longer for people to change behavioral patterns," he says. If you give a manager an appropriate amount of time and he is still not meeting the expectations you clearly laid out, Bolton says, "you'll have to decide if their continued performance is worth the price your business pays for the status quo."

Reprint U0403D

Consequences

The Secret to Holding
People Accountable

· · ·

Lila Booth

Holding employees accountable for their actions is one of a manager's most bedeviling tasks. The tendency is either to take the path of least resistance or to be vindictive. When someone doesn't come through on his commitment, we often shrink away from imposing the negative consequences, even if they've been announced well in advance, and end up harboring resentment against the person. When we do apply the negative consequences, it's all too easy to impose them as a means of humiliating the other person instead of improving performance.

Current economic conditions only complicate the situation: with many companies in financial straits, there's little room for slippage. As Owen Farren, chairman and CEO of SL Industries, a technology conglomerate with five division presidents, observes, "In an organization like ours, each president is accountable to the others. If the consequence is a greater stock price, all the businesses are able to grow, but when one company doesn't do well, it lets all the companies down." Simply put, companies are giving a gimlet eye on anything less than total achievement of the objectives you've committed yourself to—the good old college try isn't enough. As Mark Hansen, chairman and CEO of Fleming, a leading procurement and distribution company, says, "There is often confusion between efforts and results. Giving it your best try doesn't count—producing is what matters."

Precisely because managers find it uncomfortable to hold employees to their commitments—and because struggling companies can't afford for them not to—I've found, in my work as an executive coach, that a framework for building accountability into performance agreements can be extremely valuable. This framework is an iterative process for helping individuals and teams define goals, commit to specific outcomes, monitor performance, and apply the consequences.

Step #1: Drafting an Agreement

In a written document, the employee and the manager to whom he is accountable lay out the employee's targets and objectives, based on company and unit goals and the abilities of the employee. Spell out the likely positive consequences—for example, financial rewards and coveted job assignments—of excellent performance, and also the negative consequences that would accompany unsatisfactory performance. There should be no surprises.

Step #2: Monitoring Performance

Make time for regular, outcomes-based discussions of the employee's performance. Such conversations might begin as follows: "As a result of what you did, the impact on your team, on the department, on our customers, and on the company was. . . ." Supply anecdotal evidence wherever you can—the examples you cite will help cement your advice in the employee's mind.

Step #3: Applying the Consequences

"Accountability is a daily issue," says Scott Schuff, CEO of Schuff Steel. When you've got a written agreement and are having regular conversations about performance, applying the consequences becomes a less anxiety-ridden affair (although imposing negative consequences will never be easy). But don't forget the positive consequences; failure to reward successful performance is just as serious an omission as letting poor performance slide. In fact, overlooking an employee's accomplishments sends the message that what he does doesn't matter. Don't be surprised if his performance falls off as a result.

Step #4: Updating Performance Expectations

Revisions should occur regularly—whenever unit or company goals are reviewed. These updates are not substitutes for the ongoing analysis described in step #2. Rather, they're opportunities for the manager and the employee to reexamine objectives in the light of altered strategies.

> Managers often find it difficult to hold employees to their commitments—but struggling companies can't afford for them not to.

This framework for linking consequences to objectives, like most enduring challenges, is simple—deceptively simple. One thing is for certain: To convince your direct reports of the need for accountability, you and your peers must hold yourselves to the same standards. Cultures of corporate accountability thrive when managers at all levels model the desired behavior. The current climate demands nothing less.

Reprint U0109F

Are *You* Causing Problem Behavior?

. . .

It's a hard-to-swallow fact—but it's undeniable. Even seasoned managers can sometimes inadvertently cause difficult behavior in others. How? Perhaps a manager chooses to avoid a conflict with a difficult person because he or she finds it painful or uncomfortable—thus unintentionally escalating the problem behavior. Or that manager doesn't know when it's time to walk away from a "fight" and let the individuals involved resolve the situation on their own. Or that same manager may make inaccurate assumptions about feedback—for example, framing feedback in terms such as "Mistakes are crimes to be covered up"—that prevent people from learning from their problem behaviors and correcting them.

The articles in this second section present valuable wisdom on how to examine your own behaviors and attitudes, making it possible for you to then determine whether you're contributing to problem behavior in your workplace. All of this exploration takes patience, courage, and self-reflection, but you'll find plenty of recommendations for going through the process in the following pages.

Don't Avoid Conflicts— Manage Them

• • •

Monci J. Williams

Conflict on the horizon? Got a good reason for taking the easy way out?

Well of course we do. The lady in the Lennon-McCartney lyric had a character flaw: She was "a day tripper," someone who avoided entanglement by skipping out. When it comes to conflict and its avoidance, we each have our own reasons. There are people and institutional issues that will—if we let them—soak up our time and attention like a sponge. Most of us are hard-wired to experience tension at even the whiff of trouble, a reflex that prepares us to fight or flee when threatened. And any obstacle between us and the 63 tasks we must complete by Friday (no, Thursday; it's a short week) looms as an annoyance. So we do have a good reason for taking the easy way out: It's expedient.

Or so we think. But here comes (yet) another important insight in the life of a Post-Modern Manager, one that may enable him or her to make a quantum leap in productivity and effectiveness. Ducking conflict, say the experts, may actually make it harder for us to achieve our goals.

Conflict arises from people's needs, and needs unmet do not go away. They just lie in wait for the next opportunity to express themselves, which in organizational life usually means they will continue to get in the way of something we want or need to get done. Says Ellen Raider, director of training in the International Center for Cooperation and Conflict Resolution at Columbia University, "When conflict is rising, energy is directed away from tasks, and engaged instead in interpersonal issues. If you manage the conflict, people are freed to put their focus back on the tasks."

Edna Adler, a colleague of Raider's who does conflict resolution training in New York City, views conflict management skills as productivity tools. "Premature agreements, made before conflict is aired and resolved, don't last," she says. Yes, a powerful manager may be able to push through a compromise that doesn't fully address long-term business issues or individual ego needs. But he—or his subordinates—will likely spend a lot of time patching up the parts of the agreement that keep coming unglued.

"There is a difference between compliance and commitment," says Raider. "When one person is compelled to a premature agreement in which his needs are not met, he is going to get you back. He may sabotage you passive-aggressively, by foot-dragging and stalling. Or he may just get you in the back."

Intramural fratricide aside, negotiating conflict is more fundamental to the work of the manager than ever. In the age of the flat organization, "managers are constantly negotiating with colleagues about rights and resources," observes Michael Wheeler, a professor of management at Harvard Business School. Wheeler co-directs the Dispute Resolution Project at the Program on Negotiation, a collaboration between Harvard, MIT, and Tufts.

Sorting out responsibilities and resources has increasingly become the work of teams. But consultants, academics, trainers, and battle-decorated team veterans all note that teams usually do beautifully only until they bump up against their first conflict. "For all the cheerful talk about team building," says Wheeler, "unless we find creative ways to resolve conflict, the imperative to work together can be a burden."

The best way to deal with conflict effectively is to radically change the way you think about it. Mary Parker Follett, a fabled management theorist, writer, and consultant, laid down the foundation for modern thinking about the resolution of conflict more than 60 years ago. Follett suggested we "think of conflict as neither good nor bad . . . not as warfare, but as the appearance of difference." Furthermore, Follett said, since "conflict—difference—is here in the world . . . instead of condemning it, we should set it to work for us."

Follett viewed the appearance of differences as an opportunity to improve things that weren't working. Surprisingly, and correctly, Follett said that compromise was unlikely to be the optimal solution to a problem, an observation that was echoed decades later in research on the effectiveness of collaborative versus competitive approaches to negotiation, and in management theorist Herbert A. Simon's Nobel prize–winning work on managerial decision making and "satisficing."

Again anticipating the work (and some of the buzz words) of today's consultants, Follett condemned compromise as a mediocre response, and suggested that we aim for "breakthrough" solutions in which "neither side has to sacrifice anything" and the desires of both sides are "integrated." That's sometimes easier done than one might think, as Follett illustrated with the story of a dairy cooperative that nearly fell apart because of a relatively trivial fight over delivery rituals. The creamery was built on the side of a hill, and the dairymen whose route to the dairy took them down the hill thought they should unload their milk first. The dairymen whose route took them up the hill thought their unloading should take precedence.

An expedient solution, a compromise designed to reduce the amount of time spent on conflict, might entail giving each group a chance to "go first" by alternating deliveries. It took a mediator to suggest the optimal solution: Change the position of the platform so that both groups of dairymen could "go first," unloading their milk cans at the same time.

A Path to Resolution

True, some conflicts cannot be resolved unless one party, or both, give something up. And some conflicts can never be resolved because one or more of the parties would rather fight than work things out. But if you wish to proceed from the idea that you and your partner(s) in conflict can have it all, a breakthrough solution that satisfies everyone, these additional tips from the experts should help.

What People Demand Is Not Necessarily What They Must Have

The difference between the two lies in the distinction between "positions" taken in a dispute and "underlying needs." Conflict resolution trainers use "the orange," another classic Follett example, to illustrate. A mother has two children and one orange. The children are fighting over the orange, so the mother cuts it in half and gives a half to each. But as it turned out, while one child was hungry and wanted to eat the fruit, the other child wanted only the rind, so she could make candied orange peels. Each party got half of what it wanted when both could have been fully satisfied.

The story illustrates a classic bungle in problem solving—the failure to probe for the real underlying need or want. Advice from the experts: Don't assume you understand what's going on. Find out, by asking questions, proposing alternative solutions, and exploring the responses of all parties.

Your First Job Is to Understand the Other Party

The next time you see a conflict boiling up, you may notice that both parties repeatedly assert their own needs and wishes, and tell each other why the other guy is wrong. The experts call this the "attack/defend spiral," and it's where most of us flame out.

Conflict resolution trainers recommend using neutral "opening" and "informing" statements to encourage the other person to open up. Comments such as "I know we've both been very concerned about X, but I also noticed that Y is very important to you; I'd like to understand that better" encourage the other person to talk about her concerns and wants. Get in the habit of seeing the other person's position and demands as valid.

Concentrate on Common Interests, Not Differences

Focusing first on the ways in which you are "at one" with your opponent will bring you closer to agreement. Discussing differences without defining—and returning—to common ground will widen the gap between you.

Get to Know Your Own Hot Buttons and Needs

What we bring to a conflict—suspicion, anger, the conviction we can't win—may drive the conflict in directions we become helpless to correct.

To cite an example based on a real-world situation, a male economist moved from the No. 2 slot running the economic forecasting department of a large money management firm to take over the forecasting department at a slightly smaller competitor. His new subordinate, a highly competent economist, had researched and written her forecasts with little interference from her old boss. But her new boss second-guessed every draft she gave him, and she was forced to spend hours rewriting her work. With each barrage of skeptical feedback, her irritability increased.

The two were experiencing a clash in identity needs. She had a strong need for autonomy and deep pride of authorship. But he derived a strong sense of himself from his nose for trends, and from his previous department's track records for accurate forecasting. For situations like these, Roger Fisher and William Ury, authors of *Getting to Yes*, suggest stepping back—which they call "retiring to the balcony"—to get an overview of what's really happening during a conflict.

A view from the balcony might make clear to the female economist that her new boss wasn't attacking her competence. He was, for legitimate reasons, merely asserting his own. She might explore giving him an outline before she writes her drafts, and dropping in to exchange intelligence so she can integrate his thinking into her writing.

There Are Times When Avoiding Conflict Is the Right Thing to Do

Some conflicts do dissolve with time. Some institutional issues may be bigger than you and your antagonist, resolvable only by senior management, leaving you and your colleagues to work around it.

Whether you go around a conflict or tackle it head-on, the range and desirability of the solutions you create will expand if you make a considered choice on how you respond. The work of the manager is made more complex by the diffusion of authority and competition for resources in the flat organization. But however changed, the game still belongs to those who think through what they are doing, how others are likely to react, and why.

For Further Reading

Getting to Yes: Negotiating Agreement without Giving In by Roger Fisher and William Ury (1981, Viking Penguin)

Mary Parker Follett: Prophet of Management, edited by Pauline Graham (1995, Harvard Business School Press)

No Contest: The Case Against Competition by Alfie Kohn (1992, Houghton Mifflin)

Reprint U9707A

How to Handle Difficult Behaviors

• • •

Ken Cloke and Joan Goldsmith

Think of the most difficult person in your organization—yes, the one who popped into your mind the minute you read these words. Maybe it's the woman who shoots down every new idea, or the guy who's always angry and complaining. If you can learn to work productively with this person, we think you'll experience a transformation—and not only in the immediate situation but in your ability to work with anyone, anywhere.

To begin, try changing how you define the problem. Everybody talks about "difficult people" and "difficult personalities." But labeling individuals like that shifts attention from what they did to who they are. Define the problem as a *person* and you're in trouble: Your only remedy is to fire the offender (often impossible or illegal) or send him elsewhere (to become someone else's problem). By contrast, if you define the problem as difficult *behavior*, you can do something about it. People can't change who they are, but nearly everyone can change the way they act.

> Define the problem as a *person* and you're in trouble; define it as a *behavior* and you can do something.

Think, for example, of meetings you've been in, where people are personally attacking one another. If a facilitator gets consensus on ground rules banning personal attacks, the same people are likely to work together more effectively. We watched a team of managers trying to reach agreement on the design of a change process. One person refused to go along with the group, and her "difficult behavior" created conflict. But she persisted, until group members realized there was indeed a flaw in their design.

Questions to Ask

Every difficult behavior represents a question that hasn't been asked, and the answer to this question suggests a strategy for stopping it.

What makes the behavior difficult for *me*?

Often, problematic behaviors trigger issues we're sensitive to, or provoke reactions inappropriate to the situation. Maybe a troublesome colleague reminds you of a troublesome family member.

What effect has my response had on their behavior?

Negative responses can reinforce difficult behaviors. If you're dealing with an employee who has a poor self-image, she may actually need your criticism or rejection to remind her that she can't accomplish anything.

Is the behavior a way of coping with a dysfunctional system?

Ask whether there's any truth behind a colleague's criticisms or negative actions. When organizations don't encourage input, people naturally feel they have to shout to be heard.

Is the organization somehow rewarding negative behavior?

Most organizations provide substantial payoffs for dysfunctional behavior. They make concessions. They let complainers control group decisions. They even promote difficult employees just to get rid of them.

Strategies for Addressing Difficult Behaviors

Understanding the situation allows you to be softer on the person and harder on the problem.

Get it out in the open.

Ask team members to evaluate their actions on a checklist of positive and negative behaviors. Identify those they need to develop, minimize, or eliminate.

Agree on ground rules for communication.

In a work group, ask members to set simple ground rules, such as no personal insults allowed.

Act promptly . . .

When something negative is happening, interrupt the behavior and ask whether the conversation is working. People know it isn't.

. . . and frequently.

People who have been "rewarded" for difficult behaviors need ongoing support to change their patterns—regular feedback, coaching, and problem solving.

As managers shift from blaming people to solving problems, they create healthier organizations. They also learn how to transform difficult behaviors into opportunities for continued organizational growth and enhanced personal effectiveness.

Reprint U0001C

When to Walk Away from a Fight

* * *

Rebecca M. Saunders

Dennis, a sales rep, and Nancy, a marketing manager, are shouting at each other. Their argument stems from a client's complaint. The client saw a story about a competitor on the firm's Web site and told Dennis he wants it removed—*immediately*. After all, Dennis promised him exclusivity.

But Nancy refuses to remove the story. She hopes to get business from the other firm. After all, times are tough. She points out to everyone that Dennis had no right to promise exclusivity. Which is true.

The next day, Dennis has the story removed without Nancy's approval. The disagreement escalates. Dennis and Nancy snipe at each other via e-mail, and then the entire staff gets involved as the combatants defend their positions.

Sound familiar? This kind of sniping takes place every day in our high-stress, rapid-fire business climate. When people are tense and hurried, everything can seem like a crisis.

> ## If the other person is fidgeting, leaning forward, or shaking a finger in your face, then back off politely.

Ironically, the situation as described would most likely have no real impact on the bottom line. The advertising client probably wouldn't kill the current ad, exclusivity or not, nor would removing the story from the Web site discourage the other prospect from advertising.

Even so, when left unresolved, situations like this can grow into full-blown conflicts. If both parties insist they are right and refuse to back down, the cost can be high— angry words and hard feelings that never go away can make the workplace unpleasant for everyone. According to Stewart Levine, founder of ResolutionWorks and author of *Getting to Resolution: Turning Conflict into Collab-*

oration, the desire to win a disagreement, no matter how insignificant, can create a "dominance mindset" that can be greater than the issue itself.

Daniel J. Canary, another expert on interpersonal conflicts, says the issue at the center of an argument can't be as important as the damage to relationships and self-esteem that may follow. Canary, coauthor (with William R. Cupach) of *Competence in Interpersonal Conflict,* says that too often people forget that their interactions involve questions about their relationships with their peers, as well as issues about their own "identity management" (e.g., questions about self-image: Are we competent, likeable, powerful, or insignificant?). A disagreement about an issue may actually be more about someone trying to establish a dominant position, says Canary, professor of human communication at Arizona State University in Phoenix.

So when you become involved in a ground-level conflict, take a deep breath and decide if it is worth escalating or not. Here are a few tips to guide your thinking.

Calculate the Emotional Investment

Pause and ask yourself how much it would really matter—to the organization and/or yourself—if you won this difference of opinion. BJ Gallagher Hateley, of Peacock Productions in Los Angeles and coauthor (with Warren H. Schmidt) of the book *Is It Always Right to Be Right?,* says, "We can get so caught up in a disagreement that we

Watch Your Language

Some phrases can escalate difference of opinion into a conflict—and others can take a tiff and turn it into a discussion of different viewpoints. According to BJ Gallagher Hateley, coauthor (with Warren H. Schmidt) of the book *Is It Always Right to Be Right?*, phrases that can escalate conflict include:

> "How can you suggest that . . . ?"
> "Anybody can see that. . . ."
> "You can't be serious."

To facilitate communication, consider these phrases:

> "Let me see if I understand your position. . . ."
> "We both are trying to achieve but in different ways. Maybe if we . . . ."
> "I heard what you said—I want to see if I have it right."

lose sight about what winning might cost—including the trust of another, vindictiveness, self-righteousness." It doesn't make sense to let a small difference alienate a coworker and even fractionalize the department, says Levine. This is what happened in the competitor-on-the-Web situation described above, which recently occurred at a real company. With no real dollars in jeopardy, the division head ignored the situation, unaware of the impact on office productivity as staff took sides.

Stay Calm

Dennis fits the description of what Gary S. Topchik, author of *Managing Workplace Negativity,* calls a "locomotive." Locomotives take out their frustrations by steamrolling over people. When dealing with a locomotive, it's useless to try to overpower him. Rather than attack in turn, says Topchik, Nancy would have been better advised to say, "We can't get anywhere while we are shouting at each other." If the other party seemed still intent on steamrolling, then the best recourse would have been to get out of his way—over the short term. Trying to outshout the shouter would help nothing.

Be Alert to Nonverbal Signals

Facial expressions and physical gestures can tell you if the other party is in a mood to settle the difference in a collegial manner, says Deborah Borisoff, professor of speech and interpersonal communication at New York University's School of Education. For instance, if the other person is fidgeting, leaning forward, or shaking a finger in your face, says Borisoff, then back off politely. Borisoff, who is also coauthor (with David A. Victor) of *Conflict Management: A Communication Skills Approach,* advises that under these circumstances you suggest a "time out" before trying to reach a decision.

Be Assertive

If the other party tries to outshout you, says Topchik, "assume an assertive style. Give feedback on the other party's behavior. Tell them it isn't acceptable. Specify how you need to be communicated to, then redirect the discussion to the issue at hand." Don't let the issue escalate by telling everyone in your group who said what—that only spurs the other party further to prove he is right.

Tell Your Story

Let's assume you called a time out. Once you have calmed down, "tell your story and listen to the other person's." Says Levine, "Telling our story or side of a disagreement serves an essential, cathartic purpose." It is a "great information-gathering vehicle for all concerned, including the storyteller who may learn from listening to his or her own side of the difference."

Seek Information

This isn't always going to be easy, Canary says, since the other party may be keener on reinforcing his or her relationship or identity with you than talking about this single difference in opinion. However, if you can put your own viewpoint on the back burner and listen fully and effectively, says Borisoff, you may be able to come up with a resolution that satisfies you both. Levine adds: "You may also create a climate in which you or the other party are able to open up sufficiently to put problems with the relationship or identity on the table, the real issues at the source of the conflict." A smart supervisor might intervene when such situations develop. Bringing both parties into the office to question them about the dispute can create an environment in which subtler differences may become evident.

Keep in Mind That You Can't Undo What You Do

Says Canary, "Avoid short-term miscommunications." Little misunderstandings can lead to "long-term grudges. Instead, hold your own counsel." When you speak, he continues, speak calmly. There may have been past disagreements, but "take a deep breath before unloading on your peer, no matter the temptation to tell her what you think of her."

Focus on the Present and Future

If Dennis had not granted the client exclusivity, the problem would not have occurred. But hindsight won't change anything, as Topchik observes. Focus should be on the present—to resolve the current dilemma—and on the future—to avoid situations in which people don't know what their coworkers are doing. For instance, in the situation above, had Nancy known about the exclusivity clause, then she wouldn't have sought out another client in the same field, says Topchik. Better communications between the two coworkers might prevent a repetition of the situation.

> If you negotiate interests—rather than debate positions—you should come up with a fair resolution of your difference of opinion.

Reach Agreement

If you negotiate interests—rather than debate positions—you should come up with a fair resolution of your difference of opinion, in Levine's view. More important, the "agreement reached should be a shared vision of the future." As such, "it is a promise not only about resolution of the current dispute but also how future differences will be addressed."

For Further Reading

Competence in Interpersonal Conflict by William R. Cupach and Daniel J. Canary (2000, Waveland Press, Inc.)

Conflict Management: A Communication Skills Approach by Deborah Borisoff and David A. Victor (1997, Allyn & Bacon)

Getting to Resolution: Turning Conflict into Collaboration by Stewart Levine (1998, Berrett-Koehler)

Managing Workplace Negativity by Gary S. Topchik (2000, AMACOM)

Is It Always Right to Be Right? by BJ Gallagher Hateley and Warren H. Schmidt (2001, AMACOM)

Reprint C0108C

Five Questions About Business/Personal Relationships with Ronna Lichtenberg

• • •

Is it possible to have a genuine friendship with a colleague or a business partner? For many people, mixing cool, analytical thinking about how to succeed in their job with warm personal feelings toward a coworker makes for too volatile a situation. But Ronna Lichtenberg, president of the management consulting firm Clear Peak Communications, thinks it can be done.

Business success depends on your ability to bring the full richness and power of your personality to bear on your relationships with coworkers, clients, and business partners, she insisted in a recent interview. In multiple-role relationships that combine business and personal ties, however, you have to be exquisitely attentive to boundary issues—or else you'll pay a heavy price.

1. Is making a personal connection more critical to success today?

Today's large organizations are so heavily matrixed that the formal processes for getting things done are collapsing under the weight of all the demands placed on them. You almost have to have personal connections—strategic alliances with buddies in other departments—in order to accomplish anything. The big mistake being made more often now is that everyone is in constant contact via BlackBerries and cell phones, but they're focusing exclusively on tasks and not making the necessary positive connections.

2. What does "making business personal" mean?

A president of a major book publisher once told me that her company is like the old movie studios in that it takes care of its authors' needs, whatever they are. She gets involved in her authors' personal lives because she sees it as her job to decrease their burden. That's a good example of making business personal. It doesn't mean trying to make friends out of your closest business relationships. It means bringing all the nuance and intensity and charm of your personality into those relationships as a way to improve performance.

3. Does "personalizing a business relationship" lead to trouble?

When you make business personal, you put the focus on your business colleague. The more you can accommodate the way he or she learns and relates to others, the more likely you are to get good performance and collaboration out of that relationship.

Personalizing a business relationship is the opposite: It's putting the focus on *your* needs. When you do this, you're more likely to get trapped in unproductive feelings—for example, to get caught up in a perceived slight—and to disengage emotionally from the organization.

4. How can authentic friendship survive a business relationship?

First, you need to realize that whenever someone has the power to influence your financial life (directly or indirectly), a business relationship exists. Regardless of whatever else may exist between the two of you—a friendship or even a romance—the business relationship must take precedence. To put relationships ahead of performance in a work environment is going to hurt you, and it's going to hurt the other person.

To ensure that you're putting performance first, carefully delineate role responsibilities, because the requirement for mutual respect is more stringent for an office friendship than for an outside friendship. For example, some people decide that they can have genuine friendships only with people in positions not directly involved with theirs or only with people who'll never be competing with them for the same job or the same business.

Friends in a business relationship should also agree on confidentiality issues—what work-related information they must keep from each other.

People who succeed at multiple-role relationships almost always send signals, conscious or otherwise, when they want to move from one role to another. And even if things are going swimmingly, they continue to assess where the boundaries are, searching for areas of friction between their business roles and their personal roles.

5. Are there signs that a multiple-role relationship is hampering business effectiveness?

Watch for changes in pattern—for example, if the other person suddenly withdraws, seems to want to spend less time with you, becomes more aggressive, or starts asking to have a third party involved. If you notice any of these signs, it's your responsibility to initiate a conversation about role and performance expectations.

Reprint U0402D

The Four Myths of Feedback

• • •

Jamie Higgins and Diana Smith

Feedback is like exercise: we know it's good for us, but we don't do it often enough to reap the benefits. Why? When you're on the receiving end of feedback, it can be hard to remain open and receptive. Giving feedback isn't any easier. You may worry about making the other person defensive; you may fear damaging an important relationship. When it comes to feedback, who knows whether it's better to give or to receive? Neither is a picnic.

The Four Myths

As consultants, we have worked with scores of executives, and we have found that the biggest obstacles to

85

constructive feedback are some myths about feedback itself. When executives abandon these misconceptions, they find that feedback is both a lot less frightening and a lot more fruitful.

Myth 1: My reality is *the* reality, and my job is to get you to see it.

If I'm giving you feedback, I sit you down and tell you as clearly as I can what you're doing wrong. I assume that my reality is *the* reality—and that I must somehow get you to see it, either by hammering home point after point or by softly repeating the same things over and over. But a funny thing happens along the way. You balk. You feel I've missed something. You believe you can't do what I suggest given what you're up against. I say one thing; you say another. I'm selling; you're not buying. In the end you may salute, but the problem is apt to recur.

Astute executives don't buy this myth. They realize that their view is always partial, and they're more interested in getting it right than in being right. So they make a point of inquiring into the other person's views.

Myth 2: Defensiveness is bad and should be avoided at all costs.

As soon as someone differs with your feedback or suggests you might be missing something, you probably think, "Oh, boy, here we go, he's getting defensive." Then you either back down and soften the blow, thus diluting the impact (and value) of the feedback, or you ramp up your efforts in hopes that your airtight logic will overcome any defenses.

What we have found, however, is that every action to avoid or overcome defenses triggers an equal and opposite reaction. The more you push, the more the feedback-receivers push back. And they'll continue to push until what they hear takes into account the reality they see. So again: instead of discounting or trying to overcome their concerns, you might try asking more about the obstacles they face, and offer advice about how to tackle them.

Myth 3: This performance problem has nothing to do with me.

Most of us assume that the cause of whatever problems exist lies with the other person. But it isn't always the case—and executives who recognize that they might be implicated make a point of asking questions specifically about their role. We heard one executive unhappy with the timing of a project ask her subordinate, "To what extent have I made it difficult to get the project done on time?" and, "Is there anything I could be doing differently?" She then listened for what *she* had to learn.

Myth 4: Mistakes are crimes to be covered up, punished, or both.

At some level we all know this idea is wrongheaded. But if you look at how people in organizations actually behave, you'd think everyone had fallen for it. People fear that if their mistakes are uncovered they'll be tried, found guilty, and sentenced. All too often they are, in fact, punished for their mistakes, and in turn punish others.

The best companies, however, make the most of mistakes. We happened to be visiting one firm when a mistake costing several million dollars came to the attention of the CEO. "That's a significant mistake," he told the VP who had made it, "and we sure don't want it to happen again. I'd like you to identify the factors that led to the mistake and then design a system to prevent such errors in the future." Instead of covering up the error or punishing the VP for it, these executives put the mistake to work to improve the performance of the whole firm.

If you can get past these four myths, pretty soon you and the person you're giving feedback to will no longer be wrestling with each other. Instead, you'll be working side by side on a common problem. After all, the whole point of feedback is to continually improve performance. That's how you get to the Olympics. Now if we can only get to the gym.

———————

Reprint U9906E

How Should You Communicate with Difficult People?

• • •

The major weapon in your management arsenal for dealing with difficult people is your communication savvy. With skillful and effective communication, you can stave off outbursts between team members, as well as conduct disciplinary conversations in ways that lead to improved behavior in the future. You can also delicately balance the emotions, facts, and concerns about self-image that often crop up during conversations with difficult people.

In the following articles, you'll find tips and tactics for applying these valuable communication skills, as well as guidelines for how to use coaching to transform problem behavior into productive behavior. You'll also discover verbal feedback strategies that you can use to encourage future improved behavior, rather than to punish past actions.

Managing
Negativity

•　•　•

Old habits die hard. Just ask Carolyn, a manager at a Tennessee-based fabric manufacturer (she requested that her last name not be used). "The majority of our people have worked 30–35 years here, and most of them have done the same job in that time," she explains. "They get very territorial. If you come by and say, let's run the line in the other direction, it would frighten them." That fear would lead to resistance. Rumors would spread, morale would begin to sag. Before long, tardiness and absenteeism would be on the upswing.

The scenario Carolyn describes is a classic example of workplace negativity: Otherwise good employees becoming recalcitrant when forced to change their routines. But there can be other causes besides change—for example, divergent thinking styles, or a chronically difficult personality. To deal with these situations, managers must often overcome an instinctive tendency to give problem employees a wide berth. Diagnose the root causes of the negativity, advise the experts we consulted. Then focus on behaviors instead of personalities, and tackle them head-on.

Change-Induced Negativity

Often "it's not change itself, but rather how the company handles it, that results in a negative or a positive acceptance of it," says Gary Topchik, author of *Managing Workplace Negativity*. So what should you do?

Communicate the Vision

In a recent survey, 39% of respondents said management never reveals the real reason behind decisions that affect employees. When you include employees in the strategy, you help them understand the need for change. That creates buy-in.

Give Employees the Tools They Need

Helplessness breeds hopelessness. Don't let this chain reaction get started: Take an inventory of the resources and skills employees need to accomplish their new tasks, then help them acquire what's missing—quickly.

Provide a Mixture of Trust and Support

Some employees are actually eager to learn and grow in a period of change. But when they "do not get the opportunity to do so, [they] develop a negative view of their employer," says Topchik. Uncertainty abounds during times of change. Show that you have confidence in employees' ability to expand into their new roles, but be ready to offer support and advice.

When Thinking Styles Clash

Ever wonder why that intelligent, respected worker elicits sour responses from colleagues who get assigned to work with him? Sometimes the problem isn't discomfort with change, it's a mismatch of "preferred styles of thinking," says Robert M. Bramson, Ph.D., author of *Coping With Difficult People*. Bramson identifies five thinking styles:

1. SYNTHESISTS are motivated by the desire to understand;

2. IDEALISTS seek to reconcile differing opinions;

3. PRAGMATISTS prefer concrete action to analysis and theorizing;

4. ANALYSTS emphasize rational problem-solving processes; and

5. REALISTS see little need for synthesis, analysis, or compromise, because they believe the facts should be readily apparent to everyone.

Some combinations of thinking styles work better than others; otherwise positive people can turn negative when paired with an incompatible type. A synthesist, for example, is often a natural debater who loves to ponder and argue a point. "Not so much to win," Bramson explains, "but for the simple 'fun' of arguing." By contrast, a pragmatist's chief concern is "getting on with the job" and making do with what's available. When these two types are teamed up on a project, the friction can lead to negative behavior—complaints to coworkers or an unwillingness to share information and resources.

What Should You Do?

Capitalize on "creative abrasion." This term, coined by Jerry Hirshberg, head of Nissan Design International, grows out of the observation that groups often produce more and better ideas when they're composed of individuals with diverse skills, knowledge, abilities, and perspectives. In their book *When Sparks Fly,* Dorothy Leonard and Walter Swap comment on Hirshberg's practice of hiring people in pairs of opposites—for example, bringing on board an artist with a passion for colors to work alongside a designer who prefers to think logically. "This intellectual conflict Hirshberg willingly tolerated," the authors write, "believing that if the energy thus generated were channeled correctly into creativity instead of into anger, it would be a power plant of innovation."

Don't let the conflict get personalized. "It helps to be alerted to the explosive mixtures that occur when certain types of people get together," Bramson notes. "If you're aware of potential problems, you can head them off, minimize their effects, or at least get ready to duck." The key is to guide the sparks in the direction of company goals—don't allow them to set off personal attacks.

Malcontents

Back in Tennessee, Carolyn keeps a watchful eye on the few workers who "delight in putting false information out and watching it spread to see what the result is." Such people are often malcontents; they can be the most troublesome source of workplace negativity.

At one time or another, we've all been difficult to get along with. But what distinguishes a malcontent, says Bramson, is that his "troublesome behavior is habitual and affects most of the people with whom he comes in contact." Malcontents seem "immune to all the usual methods of communication and persuasion designed to convince them or help them to change their ways." To help you determine whether you're dealing with one,

You Don't Have to Handle the Negativity Alone

"Toxic handlers," a term introduced by University of British Columbia professors Peter Frost and Sandra Robinson, refers to those who voluntarily shoulder the weight of organizational angst and discord. Toxic handlers comfort colleagues, filter difficult messages, offer advice, and win confidences—in addition to carrying out their formal responsibilities. An informal network of toxic handlers is often hidden, yet it can be a tremendously valuable asset. Managers need to recognize and support this important work "before a crisis strikes," write Frost and Robinson in a 1999 *Harvard Business Review* article. Remember, too, that toxic handlers often pay a high price for their efforts—burnout, ulcers, even heart attacks. They need regular stress breaks and sometimes even professional help in order to function effectively.

Bramson recommends asking yourself the following questions:

- Did the person in question act differently in three similar situations?

- Am I reacting out of proportion to what the situation warrants?

- Did a particular incident trigger the troublesome behavior?

- Will direct, open discussion ease the situation?

If you answer *no* to all four questions, you've probably got a malcontent on your hands. When dealing with such individuals, says Bramson, your inclination to confront their attitudes directly is misguided. Their attitudes have been built up and reinforced over a lifetime. So try not to personalize them—they reflect these past encounters more than they do anything about you.

"Effective Coping"

Whether you're managing a malcontent, someone with a divergent thinking style, or a worker who is unsettled by change, don't expect to be able to change personalities, counsels Bramson. But that doesn't mean you have to allow negative behavior to go unchallenged. According to some estimates, more than 80% of those who are considered troublesome by their colleagues don't think they're being negative. In all likelihood, they've never been called on their behavior.

Bramson's recommended approach, "effective coping," is the "sum of those actions that you can take to right the power balance, to minimize the impact of others' difficult behavior in the immediate situation."

Address Only Behaviors You Can Pinpoint

For example, being late for meetings, criticizing coworkers, or spreading false rumors (be prepared to cite specific instances). But if the behavior has no perceptible effect on morale, productivity, or some other performance measure, you should leave it alone, says Topchick. After all, it could simply be a reflection of divergent thinking styles.

Acknowledge Underlying Causes

Workplace negativity can originate in sources as varied as family strife or a perceived lack of opportunity at work. When addressing such causes, be a guide rather than an instructor. Restrict your role to asking questions—avoid directives to ensure that the individual learns from the experience.

Establish Accountability

Treat negativity like any other performance measure, and hold the negativist responsible for improving his or her behavior. Together, agree on a set of ground rules you can use to measure progress.

Give Regular Feedback

In *Resolving Conflicts at Work,* authors Kenneth Cloke and Joan Goldsmith suggest that you start by "giving yourself feedback, then invite the other person or members of the group to respond. In this way, you indicate the level of honesty and nondefensiveness you expect from them, and your feedback will be received more openly." Keep the feedback constructive, specific, and fair, and deliver without a judgmental tone.

Above all, try not to engage in wishful thinking. Don't expect to be able to eliminate workplace negativity entirely. But don't delude yourself into thinking that it will vanish of its own accord, either. Managing negative behavior is a constant struggle, acknowledge Cloke and Goldsmith, but your ability to bear up under it improves when you regard it as an opportunity for "growth, resolution, and transformation."

For Further Reading

"The Toxic Handler: Organizational Hero—and Casualty" by Peter Frost and Sandra Robinson (*Harvard Business Review*, July–August 1999)

Coping with Difficult People by Robert M. Bramson, Ph.D. (1981, Dell Publishing)

Managing Workplace Negativity by Gary S. Topchik (2000, AMACOM)

Resolving Conflicts at Work by Kenneth Cloke and Joan Goldsmith (2000, Jossey-Bass)

When Sparks Fly: Igniting Creativity in Groups by Dorothy A. Leonard and Walter C. Swap (1999, Harvard Business School Press)

Reprint U0012B

Checklist for Conducting a Disciplinary Conversation

* * *

Edward Prewitt

Almost inevitably, one or more of the people who report to you will act in an unacceptable way. An hourly worker is repeatedly late; a service rep blows up at a customer; a manager makes an inappropriate comment to a subordinate. Occasionally, such actions are so egregious that the offending employee must be summarily fired. Far more often, though, the faulty behavior doesn't call for that extreme step, but it's up to the manager to dole out a measure of discipline.

The first thing to be clear about here is what you intend to achieve. Should the goal of company disciplinary policies be to punish, to mete out some form of justice? Or instead should it be to propel employees toward better behavior? Consider that the words "discipline" and "disciple" share an etymological root focused on teaching or molding. As opposed to dealing with the occasional outrageous offender, the more common challenge for managers is to use a disciplinary conversation to foster improvement in a worker who has made a mistake.

Before a Problem Occurs

Give credit when due.

The first prerequisite for a productive disciplinary conversation is that it be an exception to the usual pattern of praise and recognition. Put another way: Disciplinary actions should be only a small number of a manager's formal contacts with employees. Most workers are competent, well intentioned, and self-disciplined. If you provide feedback only, or even primarily, when they stumble, you're missing out on a signal opportunity to motivate them. Psychologists have long known that positive reinforcement is the most effective method of affecting conduct. Make a point to tell employees they've done something right—even if that something is relatively minor. Do it right after the commendable act, and do it regularly.

If they're consistently performing below your expectations, let them know.

It might seem obvious to you, the manager, that an employee's performance is subpar—but does the employee know it? In the absence of regular feedback and suggestions for how to improve, many people tend to believe they're better than they truly are. A recent study found that fully 80% of American men thought they were in the top 10% of all men when it came to athletic ability.

Communicate company rules well in advance.

Too often, management prefers to leave its disciplinary policy unspoken, perhaps fearing it will appear unfriendly and overly ready to penalize. But the majority of employees, who will never be disciplined, may actually be heartened to know that there are some boundaries you don't step over. If they perceive that the company will act firmly in the face of poor behavior, they may be relieved that they won't have to carry the load for goof-offs.

When a Problem Occurs

Don't act when you are angry.

Strong emotions cloud judgment. What's more, angry accusations beget an angry response, which turns the employee's focus away from his actions (or lack thereof) and toward the manager's response.

Reprimand in private.

Most people fear public embarrassment more than discipline itself. If you publicly injure an employee's reputation, you reduce the likelihood that her performance will improve.

Probe to determine whether the problem is with the employee or with the working conditions.

Conditions that interfere with someone's ability to do his job are often difficult to detect simply because we're so used to them. But a bit of reengineering might succeed in freeing up an employee to perform well. Ask if anything is hindering his work. This line of questioning demonstrates that you're interested in performance, not blame.

Frame your complaint specifically, in terms of observed behavior.

Lay out the difference between desired and actual behavior in a clear and unambiguous statement, and present it to the employee for discussion. This statement of the problem should be inarguable, so that the dialogue will center on identifiable actions on the part of the employee. For example, don't describe the problem as "a bad attitude"—and don't assume that's the case. A manager cannot know what goes on in an employee's head (nor can she make an accusation about attitudes stick as a defense in a suit for wrongful termination). But you can observe behavior to determine if it improves, worsens, or stays the same.

Cite the business reasons behind a policy.

If an employee tries to rationalize a transgression as "no big deal," you should be able to defend the sound business grounds for a company's policy—for example, the impact on profitability, fellow employees, or departmental deadlines. If you are unable to do so, perhaps the policy is at fault, not the employee.

Gain the employee's commitment to change.

Ask for the employee's agreement to improve her behavior. Most employees will make this commitment once their shortcomings are confronted in a calm, professional manner. If she resists, reiterate the reasons behind company policy. A personal pledge is more effective and more lasting than a boss's decree to "shape up." Furthermore, by gaining a commitment to change, you shift the focus of any future discussions from company policy to personal integrity. Straying from the latter is much more difficult to explain away.

Coach—but don't counsel.

In a disciplinary conversation, what you're trying to do is to coach the employee to improve his performance by clarifying expectations and making him understand his responsibility to act correctly. Counseling him on his personal problems is entirely different and should be left to professionals.

If a Problem Remains

Sometimes an employee will fail to improve, or will backslide. The following actions up the ante and can ultimately lead to a justified and defensible termination. Yet they also leave the door open for a change of heart on the part of the employee and permanent improvement in behavior.

Issue an oral reminder.

Meet with the employee to remind her of her promise to change. Be specific both in describing her failure to live up to that commitment and the company's expectations of performance. Be sure to state that this is the first step of the formal disciplinary process, and outline subsequent stages. Also be sure to document the meeting afterward, its spoken nature notwithstanding.

Proceed to a written reminder.

In essence, repeat the meeting in which you delivered the oral reminder, adding the facts of the continuing bad behavior and explaining that documentation of this meeting will go on permanent file. A copy should be given to the employee, along with an explicit description of what happens next. Rather than issuing a preprinted "turkey ticket," write a memo after the meeting describing your specific concerns, the steps taken thus far, and the employee's response.

Consider having the employee take a paid leave of absence.

Many companies have instituted a one-day leave of absence—with pay—at this stage in the disciplinary process. You might ask: Why pay for continued poor behavior? This concept, originated by psychologist John Huberman two decades ago, has several advantages. It continues to focus attention on the employee's behavior. It shows the company's desire to gain improvement rather than simply punish. It can transform anger, which employees typically feel during an unpaid leave, into guilt. For these reasons, companies using paid leaves of absence have consistently found that costs associated with disciplinary procedures have dropped; employees file fewer grievances and win fewer of those they do file.

Issue an ultimatum.

A key part of Huberman's approach, which is known as "positive discipline" or "discipline without punishment," is giving employees a choice: During the leave of absence, they are told, think over the company's performance demands and either commit the very next day to meeting them, or go elsewhere. In this way, the decision-making leave, as it is termed, is a far tougher response than an unpaid probation. Instead of being able to cast a manager as the heavy, an employee is forced to take responsibility for his actions and their outcome.

Terminate.

Discharge should not be viewed as the final step of the disciplinary process. It is the failure of the process. Experience has shown that most people placed on a decision-making leave come back resolved to correct their behavior. When they do not, termination should be the inevitable consequence of that choice. A firm following the procedures above will be justified—ethically and legally—in moving intransigent employees out and moving on.

For Further Reading

Discipline Without Punishment by Dick Grote (1995, AMACOM)

Supervision: The Art of Management by George L. Frunzi and Patrick E. Savini (1997, 4th edition, Prentice-Hall)

Reprint U9706D

Performance Review Anxiety

* * *

Beverly Ballaro

Olympic figure skaters and Oscar-nominated actors aside, few people relish the prospect of having their professional performances spotlighted and judged by others. Yet those on the receiving end of job reviews might be surprised to learn that the dread can cut both ways; many managers responsible for writing evaluations view the process as an unenviable task fraught with the possibility of miscommunication and misinterpretation.

"There is nothing like a poorly executed evaluation to breed resentment on the part of an employee—and frustration on the part of a supervisor," says Kelly Robertson, vice president of sales for Art Merchandising, a company that provides designs and creates in-store merchandise displays. Robertson, who has had extensive experience on both ends of the process, says that reviewers often set themselves up for trouble out of a desire to avoid offending employee sensibilities.

"Most people are not comfortable being judged themselves and therefore tend to err on the side of caution when they have to put their personal assessment of a colleague in writing," says Robertson. "What they don't realize is that an excess of diplomacy can actually produce consequences just as damaging as those created by an unduly harsh approach. By squandering an opportunity to deliver meaningful criticism, they deprive both themselves and the employees they are evaluating of any practical benefits. They turn the process into an exercise in futility, and a time-consuming one at that."

The tricky part, of course, lies in mastering the delicate balancing act essential to packaging a meaningful assessment in terms palatable enough that the review can effect real change. Valid criticism accomplishes no purpose if it falls on deaf, alienated ears. To make sure your message comes through soft and clear, you need to cultivate a perspective that is firm yet flexible, critical yet encouraging, honest yet polite, personal yet professional. Although this may sound like a mission near impossible for many managers, the challenge is not as insurmountable as you might think.

Bear in mind that the guiding tenet behind successful comedy, opera, and baseball also holds true for fair and effective performance reviews: it really is, as the saying goes, all in the delivery. Not just the substance of what you write but especially how you write it can spell the crucial difference between a productive, motivational critique and a recipe for simmering resentment.

Accomplishments: Always Lead with Your Best Material

Even when the review is weighted toward the critical, it makes psychological sense to start out on a positive note. Acknowledging, front and center, an employee's achievements to date makes him more receptive to the

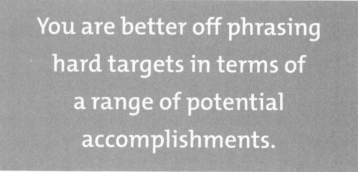

You are better off phrasing hard targets in terms of a range of potential accomplishments.

recommendations for improvement that follow. Tying the accomplishments to specific challenges set forth previously—in the employee's last evaluation, for example—provides objective, tangible evidence of progress. It also creates a sense of fair play, as the employee understands in advance the specific criteria by which he is being assessed.

While you want to communicate your standards of judgment unambiguously, at the same time you want to recognize that the value of an employee stems from more than what you can summarize with numbers and checklists. It is therefore wise to combine specific accomplishments—*With final revenues totaling $750,000 for fiscal year 2002, Jim exceeded the goal set last January by 27%*—with more general character-based accolades:

> Mark's outperformance of sales expectations is all the more impressive given the weak economic environment in which we are operating. His perseverance and spirit of innovation propelled him to look outside the box of the company's traditional client base for new customers. His willingness to leave no stone unturned should serve as a model to his peers.

By acknowledging not just the results generated but also the personality traits and behaviors that made those results possible, you generate a more individualized message of praise and, ultimately, greater pride and incentive on the part of the employee.

Goals: The Sky's Not the Limit

Once you have established a reservoir of goodwill by homing in on an employee's accomplishments, you should capitalize on that momentum by staking out realistic targets for the next evaluation phase. The language you use to describe these targets should reflect a blend of specific, quantifiable objectives with more abstract, character-driven aims. You are better off phrasing hard targets in terms of a range of potential accomplishments—*Dana will increase sales between 10% and 20%*—rather than hitching them to narrow benchmarks: *Philip will bring in $1.5 million worth of new business.* By writing flexibility into the expectations, you give the employee psychological breathing room. You also provide her with an incentive to outperform expectations rather than setting her up for falling short of the mark.

The generic aims should be tied to traits and behaviors that will help your employee meet her targets. The goal here is to highlight behaviors in a way that reinforces a positive trend: *John will continue his aggressive pursuit of opportunities in previously untapped sectors.* Save any problematic behaviors or lack of behaviors you wish to address for the "areas to improve" section, as you don't want to taint the goals section with any hint of the negative.

Strategies: How Do We Get There from Here?

After you have identified for an employee both a range of goals and the mindset necessary to achieve them, the next logical step is to map out, in a pragmatic fashion and with employee input, different possible paths to success:

Lisa will improve order processing efficiency by making use of the tools of e-commerce.

Fred will contact all tristate-area college alumni magazines that sell classified ads.

James will oversee the implementation of the new software ordered to ensure that, by the end of FY03, all personnel records are secure and searchable online.

The idea here is to describe actions, resources, and plans of action in terms as specific as possible. Philosophical overviews belong in the concluding summary, not here, where you want to present your employee with a "nuts and bolts" repertoire of approaches that he or she can draw upon in the coming cycle.

Areas to Improve: Collaborate, Don't Assassinate

Now that you've delivered all the good news—the ways in which your employee has shone in the past year, the positive expectations you have established together for the coming year, the road map you have outlined for fulfilling those goals—the timing is opportune to raise any and all problematic issues you need to address. The key is to lay out your case in language that is straightforward yet not withering.

1. Emphasize the Positive Within the Negative

Don't write: *Mike will not delay in responding to all customer complaints in a timely and courteous fashion.* Instead, you should write: *Mike will ensure—by assuming personal responsibility for generating same-day voice or e-mail responses to all customer queries—that every client feels connected to every phase of every project.*

2. Couch Your Criticism in Terms of the Shared Greater Good

For instance, writing *Carla will commit, along with her colleagues, to divisionwide efforts to decrease backlogged work pressures by reducing the volume of personal phone calls and e-mails during working hours* is sure to generate less hostility—and better results—than writing *Carla will refrain from making personal phone calls or sending personal e-mails on company time.*

3. Enlist Your Employee As an Ally

For example, consider bringing the employee into a situation to which he can uniquely contribute.

> Steve will help me identify the best solution to the problem of meeting outsourcer-driven production deadlines by preparing status updates every Monday morning until each project is completed.

4. Offer the Employee Flexible Options in Resolving a Shortcoming

By doing so, you give the employee a sense of agency and you also make it clear that the choice is not about if the problem will be fixed but simply how this will be accomplished:

> Mark will be able to compensate for arrivals at his desk later than 8:30 A.M. through the means of his choice: He may skip his morning break, reduce his lunch hour, or depart later than the end of regular workday in order to complete all his scheduled hours.

Consequences and Incentives: Offer Carrots but Don't Be Afraid to Use a Stick

Now that you've spelled out in no uncertain terms what the employee is capable of, what he or she is expected to accomplish, and how to optimize his or her chances of meeting those expectations, it is reasonable to outline what the future might hold.

If the purpose of the review is to whip a largely negative job performance into shape, you should offer a note of encouragement but state unequivocally the range of possible outcomes:

It is my hope that Jennifer will take good advantage of the resources and models that have been proposed to her as a means of bringing her performance up to a level that satisfies the licensing criteria of the state and the evaluation standards of this institution. If, by the interim evaluation scheduled to take place six months from now, Jennifer is meeting a majority of the standards, she will be permitted to complete, on a probationary basis, the remainder of the work year. If, by the end of the work year, she has not demonstrated competency in all the required areas, she will not be offered another contract.

If the overall purpose of the evaluation is to heap praise on an exemplary employee, you can either skip this section entirely or focus on incentives:

Larry's role in courting and bringing into the fold our new real estate division demonstrates his potential to help this firm expand into territories in which we were not previously competitive. If he succeeds in lining up a full complement by the year's end, Larry will be the logical choice to head the division.

If the review consists, as most do, of a mixed bag of accolades and critiques, you can substitute a brief, balanced summary statement in place of the consequences section:

> Overall, I am pleased by Mary's progress toward the goals we established last year at this time. Although she needs to increase her degree of follow-up on projects, she has demonstrated excellent creativity at the conceptual stages. She is a fine asset to the company and I look forward to continuing working with her.

Remember, your goal in writing a review is to improve performance, not to punish or to dispense empty praise. Honesty, leavened with tact, will make the experience much less anxious and more productive for everyone involved.

Reprint C0310D

"I Just Can't Bring Myself to Talk About That with Her."

How to Have Difficult Conversations

• • •

Ever have trouble bringing up the matter of a raise with a hard-nosed boss? Or felt helpless when confronting a teenager who says, "Why don't you trust me?" Or delayed giving a less-than-glowing performance review to a colleague who is also a close friend?

In *Difficult Conversations: How to Discuss What Matters Most,* authors Douglas Stone, Bruce Patton, and Sheila

Heen give us a step-by-step way to handle the discussions we spend so much time dreading.

Step one, the authors say, is to sort out which conversation you're actually trying to have. Conversations take place on three different levels. First, there's the "What happened?" conversation about what is actually going on. Difficult conversations often involve substantial disagreements about the actual facts of the case. For example, was the project late because the supplier was incompetent, or were there extenuating circumstances?

Second, there's the "Feelings" conversation. Every tough talk involves feelings that are potentially painful or awkward. We need to be able to handle both the other person's feelings and our own. Does that supplier get incredibly defensive when you complain about lateness because he's a jerk, or because he's worried he will lose the contract?

And finally, there's the "Identity" conversation. Does this conversation threaten our definitions of self? No one likes to believe themselves incompetent or unlovable, and difficult conversations can involve these hard moments of self-scrutiny. Is that supplier a perfectionist who feels threatened when confronted with evidence that he's in fact less than perfect?

On the level of fact, the authors ask us to focus not on what is true, but on what is important. We usually interpret our own and others' actions differently because different things are important to us. The goal here is not to accuse the other person of lying, but to try to get out on the table what is important to each party. It is crucial here not to impute intentions to the other person—let him tell you what his intentions are. And similarly, don't fall into the blame game. That only leads to feelings of frustration and hostility on both sides.

Instead, the authors counsel us to "shift to a learning conversation." Focus on getting clear about what both parties intend, what both parties want, and, fundamentally, who both parties are. Ask that supplier what his understanding of the contract was, and whether he had all the information he needed to complete the job. Was he waiting for a crucial bit of data you were supposed to supply but got to him a little late?

At this level, moreover, you need to disentangle intention from impact. We need first to understand what the other person's intention was. Did the supplier intend to get the product to you precisely on time, or only within what he saw as an acceptable range? The only way to know is to ask. Then, we need to talk about the impact of that intention. A good intention can still have a bad impact on someone else, and both parties need to acknowledge this hard truth.

At the second level—feelings—we need to learn to describe our own feelings carefully, without merely venting, and give others the time and respect to do the same. Both parties need to avoid using the classic line that always makes good arguments go bad: "You made me feel. . . ." Talk about the way you feel, and then let the other person do the same. Don't place the blame on him.

At the identity level, we need to ask ourselves what is at stake. The authors counsel that letting go is frequently an appropriate response to situations that are not, in fact, life and death. In this way, we can make better decisions about when to raise an issue and when to simply let it go. Instead of sticking to your own story, take time to learn the other person's story of what happened—and then create a third story in which you begin by inviting the other person to explain her feelings and perception of what's at stake. Ask open-ended questions, paraphrase to check that you've understood, and acknowledge the other person's feelings. What is most important in your relationship with the supplier? On-time delivery? Or quality? Deciding on a story the two of you agree upon can lead to a more harmonious and successful working relationship.

Ultimately, the authors urge us to see conversations as not a question of "either–or," but rather "both–and." These insights will not make difficult conversations easy, alas, but they will make them more fruitful. Keep that in mind the next time your teenager asks "Why don't you trust me?"

For Further Reading

Difficult Conversations: How to Discuss What Matters Most by Douglas Stone, Bruce Patton, and Sheila Heen (1999, Viking)

Reprint C0003B

The Communication Secrets of Executive Coaches

How to Have Conversations That Lead to Action

•   •   •

Nick Morgan

It's a manager's function to coach an employee through a problem or crisis on the job. And when the crisis has been caused by the employee's own mistake, it's an opportunity for the manager to help the employee learn—and change the behavior that led to the problem.

But it's not always easy to know what to say or how to coach, especially in stressful moments. Executive coaches thrive on such moments. The field of executive coaching is growing fast; the business climate being what it is today, executives believe that they need to have every advantage possible in order to survive and, ideally, thrive in a demanding, rapidly changing environment.

Executive coaches seek to change behavior through one-on-one conversations at key moments in executives' careers. The best ones are masters of focused talk; through their conversations, or "interventions," as they sometimes call them, they look to make lasting changes in their clients' behavior.

So what can some of the top coaches teach us about *really* effective communications? How can you adapt some of their insights to your own business and personal conversations so that you know what to say and when to say it? The following executive coaching techniques first address matters of topic and timing, and then consider the habits of mind that will best enable you to communicate powerfully.

Look for Moments of Crisis

Executive coaches counsel that it does indeed take a crisis to make people want to change their behavior—or even listen to a coach. So in your communications, pick the "points of pain"—the missed deadline, the botched proposal that came back rejected—and focus on them. In an information-saturated age, people are not much interested in business conversations that don't have a strong imperative behind them. Recognize that you need to save your breath for the moments of greatest need.

Alan Downs, executive coach and author of *Secrets of an Executive Coach: Proven Methods for Helping Leaders Excel Under Pressure,* says, "Not every executive who is failing is in a crisis. Furthermore, most executives will experience crises only at critical points in their careers. The point is this: There is an optimal time in an executive's career when he is experiencing crisis and when coaching is immensely helpful." The successful manager learns to pick her moments just as the executive coach does.

Commit to Telling the Truth

This is a prerequisite to having an effective conversation about change, but it's easier said than done. "Telling the truth is a skill that may take several years to master," says Thomas J. Leonard, founder of Coach University and author of *The Portable Coach: 28 Surefire Strategies for Business and Personal Success.* "That's because telling the truth is something that doesn't always come naturally. Mark Twain wrote a great line about congressmen being people who would never lie 'unless it was absolutely convenient.' Well, we all have those same truthful-when-convenient tendencies."

But, he adds, "If you are for real, good people will want to be around you. Because even though we all want to seek and ultimately claim an optimized reality, the present-moment truth remains very, very attractive."

Have a Vision

Powerful, transforming conversations are far more likely to take place if you have a vision to impart to your listener. Visions are dynamic, attractive, and seductive. And, according to Leonard, not that difficult to develop.

> Executive coaches counsel that it takes a crisis to make people want to change their behavior.

"'Have a vision' sounds like such a big or impressive thing, doesn't it? But don't get intimidated. A vision is a very practical thing. Having a vision is just a natural extension of being who you are," he says.

People want to feel that they are involved in something larger than themselves, and if you can convey a sense of vision or mission to your listener, you will be far more likely to enroll him in your plan for change. So don't just tell your employee to go back and redo the proposal. Explain how important the proposal is to the company, and *then* tell him to go back and redo it.

Use the Appropriate Vocabulary

This is more difficult than it sounds. It means dropping pretense, jargon, "spin," and all the other ways in which we sugarcoat the sometimes hard things we need to say in order to create the right climate for change. The irony is that letting go of these devices has the effect of making you more attractive to others—because they will come to learn that they can trust you.

Engage Your Own Passion

Many businesspeople still seem to believe that business is the place where all good emotions go to die. You leave your personal life at home; work is the world of automatons.

Nothing could be further from the truth, according to the executive coaches. To the contrary, executives—and coaches—who can't or won't engage their emotions in the workplace are doomed to failure. Downs says, "Maybe you're thinking, 'Can't an executive just act one way at work and be his real self at home?'" The answer is no. "Sure, you might be able to do it for a month or even a few years, but slowly your grasp on your own values and feelings will begin to slip."

> Many businesspeople still seem to believe that business is the place where all good emotions go to die. Nothing could be further from the truth.

The process is called dissociation, and it's deadly to communications. Few businesspeople are good enough actors to communicate with apparent sincerity and conviction about something that they are not passionate about.

If you can't—or won't—be truly passionate about your business communications, then you are in the wrong business.

Ground Your Communications in Strong Relationships

A solid relationship is the basis for successful coaching, says James Flaherty, executive coach and author of *Coaching:*

Evoking Excellence in Others, and it is often the result of deliberate effort.

"Sometimes people believe that relationships are natural and either happen or don't happen, and that any interference in such a 'natural' process is a manifestation of some neurotic need to control or be in charge," he writes. "The type of relationship necessary for coaching is not one that's based upon 'chemistry.' It's more a matter of openness, communication, appreciation, fairness, and shared commitment."

Of course we like some people more than others. "This doesn't matter in coaching people, however, and it doesn't matter in building a successful coaching relationship," he says. What matters is trust.

Communicate from a Position of Awareness

Key to strong relationships are two further qualities effective communicators need to possess: awareness and self-knowledge. You need to understand the practical and psychological terrain you are working in, both your own and that of the people you are communicating with. Without self-knowledge, you will be unable to understand the limits to your own effectiveness as a communicator.

What is your power position relative to everyone else—is it one of strength or one of weakness? Are you trying to change a peer's behavior or the behavior of a direct report? Awareness is the basis for good listening, and listening is, of course, the sine qua non of effective, behavior-changing conversation.

Now turn that awareness toward yourself. Good communicators know their own blind spots and work around them. Leonard advises you to identify your worst weakness: "Are you a wimp? A liar? Insensitive? Impatient? Selfish? A dilettante? Or worse?"

Now look closely at the weakness you've identified. You'll find, he says, "something of incredible value." Think you're a wimp? Maybe you're just a supersensitive person—and that's a real gift.

"Weaknesses," he says, "can really be great signposts."

Executive coaching has flowered in recent years in part because of the perception that the competition is tougher and the stakes are higher in the workplace today than ever before. In this atmosphere, strong communication skills are all the more essential for managers who want to be able to influence the behavior of those around them.

Applying the coaches' own secrets to your communications may just save you the time and expense of hiring a coach yourself.

For Further Reading

Secrets of an Executive Coach: Proven Methods for Helping Leaders Excel Under Pressure by Alan Downs (2002, AMACOM)

Coaching: Evoking Excellence in Others by James Flaherty (1999, Butterworth-Heinemann)

The Portable Coach: 28 Surefire Strategies for Business and Personal Success by Thomas J. Leonard (1998, Scribner)

Reprint C0209B

Feedback in the Future Tense

* * *

Hal Plotkin

Last year, the staffing firm Kelly Services placed approximately 700,000 workers in new positions. The quality of the managerial feedback those workers received often determined their success or failure, says Steve Armstrong, the company's vice president of metro market operations. "It's absolutely at the top," he says. "Nothing good ever happens when the feedback is lacking."

This is gospel at a company that regularly solicits feedback from the corporations into which it places workers to determine how those workers did on the job.

But in many companies, feedback is something that is feared, avoided, or done halfheartedly at best. And that's a shame, because feedback is the key to unlocking the promise of continuous improvement. So how do you do it without alienating the very employees you want to help?

> If you don't listen to employees, it's less likely they will listen to you.

The answer is to begin by changing the conversation from one primarily about performance—the past—to one about change—the future. In other words, rather than blaming an employee for past mistakes, talk quite specifically about how that employee needs to improve. Give the employee a goal to work toward, not a legacy to overcome. Your ultimate goal "is to energize and excite people about the role you need them to play and the development they need to go through," observes Charles H. Bishop, Jr., in *Making Change Happen One Person at a Time.*

Managers and HR people need to assess employees' change capacity and not just their performance, says Bishop. When employees understand that they are expected to strive for continuous improvement, they are far more likely to take positive action as a result of feedback rather than resist it.

Not all employees embrace change; indeed, many are uncomfortable with it, and some actively resist it. It is essential that you, as their manager, communicate the high value your organization places on a willingness to change and improve.

When it is understood in that context, feedback becomes a welcome tool employees can use to achieve their own goals for advancement and recognition rather than an event to be dreaded. Formal, semiannual performance reviews provide an ideal vehicle with which to initiate or reinvigorate the feedback loop.

Facilitate Feedback with a Six-Step Process

"If you do your job correctly, there will be sufficient ongoing communication so that all your employees know what is expected of them and how well or poorly they are doing," write Jack H. Grossman and J. Robert Parkinson in *Becoming a Successful Manager*. They recommend a six-step approach to facilitate feedback.

1. Identify Successes and Failures

Be specific. Don't tell an employee he is late too often. Instead, tell him the exact number of times he has been late during a defined period.

Be equally specific when offering praise, such as the amount of money or time a worker has saved the company. When talking with an employee, suggest Grossman and Parkinson, "focus on the actions rather than on your conclusions."

Indeed, one of the biggest mistakes a manager can make is to overlook the importance of giving feedback to valued workers. No one likes to feel unappreciated. Roughly 25% of good employees who quit left due to lack of recognition, according to a 1998 survey by Robert Half International. Give too little feedback to your best workers and they may take their talents elsewhere.

Giving feedback to difficult employees requires an even greater degree of skill and sensitivity. In these situations, managers should keep in mind the distinction between factual and emotional feedback. Expressing anger or disappointment with the employee, either verbally or nonverbally, can be counterproductive.

In short, try to avoid letting your emotions get in the way. Instead, stick to discussing the specific behaviors at issue. And remember that communication is more than words: it's also body language, facial expressions, and tone of voice. The wrong moves in any of these areas can exacerbate problem behavior by turning feedback sessions into confrontations rather than constructive and productive exchanges.

"If you try to deliver some factual feedback but your nonverbal signals indicate you are very angry, then the person is more likely to react with defensiveness or aggression," observes Robert Bacal in *Dealing with Difficult Employees.*

2. Stop Talking and Start Listening

Ask employees to respond to your observations and pay careful attention to their words and body language; ask questions as necessary to make sure they've had a full opportunity to get their views across. If you don't listen to what an employee has to say, it's less likely he will listen to what you have to say.

3. Discuss the Implications of Behavior

If you are dealing with problem behavior, convey the probable outcomes in clear and unmistakable terms, such as the likelihood of being put on probation by a certain date, missing the next round of raises, or being demoted. Likewise, let performing employees know if they are on target to receive a bonus or other recognition. Specific information about consequences provides employees with benchmarks against which to assess and adjust their behavior.

A useful technique for dealing with particularly difficult employees is to take extra time to help them understand the organizational consequences of their behavior. If an employee does not return customer phone calls promptly, for example, you might show her how her conduct affects customer satisfaction ratings. Make sure she understands the reasons she is being asked to do something. Armed with such information, employees are less likely to regard feedback as arbitrary or punitive.

4. Link Past Accomplishments to Needed Changes

Look for areas where the employee has been successful and point out how the traits that led to those successes can be applied to areas that need improvement. Don't just offer exhortations; build an employee's confidence by letting him know exactly why you think he will be able to handle whatever tasks are at issue. Explain how current workplace requirements are related to his previous accomplishments.

One excellent way to convey this type of information to workers who aren't getting it is by using group feedback to augment personal feedback. This can be accomplished by creating a nonconfrontational setting, such as organizing a division or workgroup meeting where a given subject, say improving customer satisfaction ratings, is discussed with no one being put on the spot. Encourage your best workers to participate in these sessions and get them to share their ideas and practices with underperformers. Draw out the discussions so that areas of potential improvement are highlighted and reinforced by the group. Then take the problem employee aside privately after the meeting to drive home any points that may be particularly relevant to her.

"The more sources of feedback available to a difficult person," writes Bacal, the more likely it is that he or she will "actually hear and act on the messages to make improvements."

5. Agree on an Action Plan

Ask the employee what steps he can take to address issues that have been identified. Solicit his suggestions. This is "a powerful tactic because people are more likely to follow through on their own ideas than on what they are told to do by someone else," note Grossman and Parkinson.

Make sure the specific ideas, timetables, and plans are realistic—and measurable, if possible—and then write those plans down and initial them along with the employee.

6. Follow Up

Set a date and time to meet again for a formal review on progress related to the action plan. But don't wait for that date to stay engaged with the employee. Instead, use the development of the action plan as the starting point for the more regular, informal feedback sessions that distinguish a good manager. Let employees know when they are on plan and when they might be falling short.

The mystery about the timing or fairness of feedback is greatly reduced when the feedback is directly related to an agreed-upon action plan.

Keeping up this constant feedback loop in between regular sit-downs, suggest Grossman and Parkinson, also reduces the anxiety that often attends the more formal scheduled performance reviews.

Remember to Express Appreciation

You should also be creative when it comes to providing ongoing positive feedback. Words of thanks can be the starting point, but there are many other ways to get messages of appreciation across, says Barbara A. Glanz in *Handle with Care: Motivating and Retaining Employees.*

Glanz suggests managers write letters and notes of commendation and put copies in the employee's personnel files. Or give workers a night out on the town, a surprise day off, tickets to a play or concert, or a gift certificate to their favorite store or restaurant.

If all this sounds like a lot of trouble, keep the stakes in mind. "People do not quit organizations," notes Glanz. "They quit bosses."

For Further Reading

The Complete Idiot's Guide to Dealing with Difficult Employees by Robert Bacal (2000, Alpha Books)

Making Change Happen One Person at a Time: Assessing Change Capacity Within Your Organization by Charles H. Bishop, Jr. (2001, AMACOM)

Handle with Care: Motivating and Retaining Employees by Barbara A. Glanz (2002, McGraw-Hill)

Becoming a Successful Manager by Jack H. Grossman and J. Robert Parkinson (2002, Contemporary Books)

Reprint C0211A

About the Contributors

Constantine von Hoffman is a contributor to *Harvard Management Update*.

David Whitemyer writes about workplace design, managing people, and office culture.

Paul Michelman is editor of *Harvard Management Update*.

Lila Booth is an executive coach and consultant specializing in organizational culture. She teaches at the University of Pennsylvania's Wharton School of Small Business Development Center and lives in Blue Bell, Pennsylvania.

Monci J. Williams is a contributor to *Harvard Management Update*.

Ken Cloke and **Joan Goldsmith** are consultants and trainers specializing in conflict resolution, mediation, and organizational change. They are coauthors of *Resolving Conflicts at Work: A Complete Guide for Everyone on the Job*.

Rebecca M. Saunders is a management writer based in New York City.

Jamie Higgins is a senior consultant in Monitor Company, a global consulting firm based in Cambridge, Massachusetts. **Diana Smith** is a partner of Action Design and the Chair of Organizational Dynamics at Monitor University.

About the Contributors

Edward Prewitt is a contributor to *Harvard Management Update*.

Beverly Ballaro has taught language, literature, and writing courses at Yale, Cornell, and Wheelock College.

Nick Morgan is a former editor to *Harvard Management Update*.

Hal Plotkin is a writer and editor based in Palo Alto, California. The former editor of *Entrepreneur of the Year* magazine, he currently writes a regular column for the *San Francisco Chronicle*'s SFGate.com.

Harvard Business Review Paperback Series

The Harvard Business Review Paperback Series offers the best thinking on cutting-edge management ideas from the world's leading thinkers, researchers, and managers. Designed for leaders who believe in the power of ideas to change business, these books will be useful to managers at all levels of experience, but especially senior executives and general managers. In addition, this series is widely used in training and executive development programs.

Books are priced at $19.95 U.S.
Price subject to change.

Title	Product #
Harvard Business Review **Interviews with CEOs**	3294
Harvard Business Review on **Advances in Strategy**	8032
Harvard Business Review on **Becoming a High Performance Manager**	1296
Harvard Business Review on **Brand Management**	1445
Harvard Business Review on **Breakthrough Leadership**	8059
Harvard Business Review on **Breakthrough Thinking**	181X
Harvard Business Review on **Building Personal and Organizational Resilience**	2721
Harvard Business Review on **Business and the Environment**	2336
Harvard Business Review on **Change**	8842
Harvard Business Review on **Compensation**	701X
Harvard Business Review on **Corporate Ethics**	273X
Harvard Business Review on **Corporate Governance**	2379
Harvard Business Review on **Corporate Responsibility**	2748
Harvard Business Review on **Corporate Strategy**	1429
Harvard Business Review on **Crisis Management**	2352
Harvard Business Review on **Culture and Change**	8369
Harvard Business Review on **Customer Relationship Management**	6994
Harvard Business Review on **Decision Making**	5572
Harvard Business Review on **Effective Communication**	1437

Title	Product #
Harvard Business Review on **Entrepreneurship**	9105
Harvard Business Review on **Finding and Keeping the Best People**	5564
Harvard Business Review on **Innovation**	6145
Harvard Business Review on **Knowledge Management**	8818
Harvard Business Review on **Leadership**	8834
Harvard Business Review on **Leadership at the Top**	2756
Harvard Business Review on **Leading in Turbulent Times**	1806
Harvard Business Review on **Managing Diversity**	7001
Harvard Business Review on **Managing High-Tech Industries**	1828
Harvard Business Review on **Managing People**	9075
Harvard Business Review on **Managing the Value Chain**	2344
Harvard Business Review on **Managing Uncertainty**	9083
Harvard Business Review on **Managing Your Career**	1318
Harvard Business Review on **Marketing**	8040
Harvard Business Review on **Measuring Corporate Performance**	8826
Harvard Business Review on **Mergers and Acquisitions**	5556
Harvard Business Review on **Motivating People**	1326
Harvard Business Review on **Negotiation**	2360
Harvard Business Review on **Nonprofits**	9091
Harvard Business Review on **Organizational Learning**	6153
Harvard Business Review on **Strategic Alliances**	1334
Harvard Business Review on **Strategies for Growth**	8850
Harvard Business Review on **The Business Value of IT**	9121
Harvard Business Review on **The Innovative Enterprise**	130X
Harvard Business Review on **Turnarounds**	6366
Harvard Business Review on **What Makes a Leader**	6374
Harvard Business Review on **Work and Life Balance**	3286

Management Dilemmas:
Case Studies from the Pages of
Harvard Business Review

How often do you wish you could turn to a panel of experts to guide you through tough management situations? The Management Dilemmas series provides just that. Drawn from the pages of *Harvard Business Review*, each insightful volume poses several perplexing predicaments and shares the problem-solving wisdom of leading experts. Engagingly written, these solutions-oriented collections help managers make sound judgment calls when addressing everyday management dilemmas.

These books are priced at $19.95 U.S.
Price subject to change.

Harvard Business Essentials

In the fast-paced world of business today, everyone needs a personal resource—a place to go for advice, coaching, background information, or answers. The Harvard Business Essentials series fits the bill. Concise and straightforward, these books provide highly practical advice for readers at all levels of experience. Whether you are a new manager interested in expanding your skills or an experienced executive looking to stay on top, these solution-oriented books give you the reliable tips and tools you need to improve your performance and get the job done. Harvard Business Essentials titles will quickly become your constant companions and trusted guides.

These books are priced at $19.95 U.S., except as noted.
Price subject to change.

Title	Product #
Harvard Business Essentials: **Negotiation**	1113
Harvard Business Essentials: **Managing Creativity and Innovation**	1121
Harvard Business Essentials: **Managing Change and Transition**	8741
Harvard Business Essentials: **Hiring and Keeping the Best People**	875X
Harvard Business Essentials: **Finance for Managers**	8768
Harvard Business Essentials: **Business Communication**	113X
Harvard Business Essentials: **Manager's Toolkit ($24.95)**	2896
Harvard Business Essentials: **Managing Projects Large and Small**	3213
Harvard Business Essentials: **Creating Teams with an Edge**	290X

The Results-Driven Manager

The Results-Driven Manager series collects timely articles from *Harvard Management Update* and *Harvard Management Communication Letter* to help senior to middle managers sharpen their skills, increase their effectiveness, and gain a competitive edge. Presented in a concise, accessible format to save managers valuable time, these books offer authoritative insights and techniques for improving job performance and achieving immediate results.

These books are priced at $14.95 U.S.
Price subject to change.

Readers of the Results-Driven Manager series find the following Harvard Business School Press books of interest.

If you find these books useful:	You may also like these:
Presentations That Persuade and Motivate	Working the Room (8199)
Getting People on Board	
Face-to-Face Communications for Clarity and Impact	HBR on Effective Communication (1437)
Dealing with Difficult People	HBR on Managing People (9075)
Winning Negotiations That Preserve Relationships	HBR on Negotiation (2360)
	HBE Guide to Negotiation (1113)
Teams That Click	The Wisdom of Teams (3670)
	Leading Teams (3332)
Managing Yourself for the Career You Want	Primal Leadership (486X)
	Leading Quietly (4878)
Taking Control of Your Time	Leadership on the Line (4371)

How to Order

Harvard Business School Press publications are available worldwide from your local bookseller or online retailer.
You can also call

1-800-668-6780

Our product consultants are available to help you
8:00 a.m.–6:00 p.m., Monday–Friday, Eastern Time.
Outside the U.S. and Canada, call: 617-783-7450
Please call about special discounts for quantities greater than ten.

You can order online at

www.HBSPress.org